Teaching and Assessment Handbook 2
(Turquoise–Gold bands)

Contents

Welcome to Project X CODE	2
Project X CODE structure chart	3
Who Project X CODE is for	4
Project X CODE – At a glance	6
Project X CODE – A new approach	8
A new mission for Team X	10
Project X CODE and your school's provision for intervention	12
Phonic progression	13
Comprehension progression	16
A summary of progression	18
Reading enrichment	19
Moving to independence	21
Learning to spell with Project X CODE	22
The selection process for Project X CODE	23
Tracking and assessing progress	24
Following up on assessment findings	25
Determining when to leave Project X CODE	26
Project X CODE Phonic record sheets	27
Project X CODE Practice and Assessment CD-ROM	30
Project X CODE End of band progress checks	33
Comprehension checklist	36
End of band reading passages	37
Implementing Project X CODE	42
Involving parents and carers in Project X CODE	43
Project X CODE – Session notes and getting started	44
Guided reading in Project X CODE	45
Menu of activities	47
Project X CODE – Setting the scene	53
The structure of Project X CODE sessions	54
Session notes and PCMs	56

Welcome to Project X CODE

Project X CODE is an innovative reading intervention programme, which combines systematic synthetic phonics, comprehension development, motivational 3D design and gripping stories to accelerate struggling readers' progress so that children reach expected literacy levels as soon as possible.

Project X CODE is primarily aimed at children in Years 2–4 (P3–5) who have experienced a phonics programme but are falling behind in reading. It includes highly engaging books, detailed session notes, tools and software to track and assess progress, eBooks, an animation and a host of free online support materials.

At the heart of **Project X CODE** are exciting adventure books underpinned by a clear progression in systematic synthetic phonics, carefully sequenced using the familiar phonic progression found in *Letters and Sounds* and other high-quality phonic programmes. A carefully structured progression in comprehension is also followed through the series.

CODE is part of Project X, a high-quality whole-school reading programme built to motivate children and raise literacy standards.

What makes Project X CODE different?

Project X CODE incorporates all the major elements involved in learning to read successfully:

- **Decoding using systematic synthetic phonics**: the sessions focus on rapid and automatic decoding and application, building blending and segmenting skills to ensure children apply phonic skills as their first approach to reading.

- **Reading decodable texts**: each book contains two texts. The first is 100% decodable to ensure children experience success using phonemic strategies. The second is at least 80% decodable – the richer text motivates children and develops vocabulary and comprehension.

- **Developing both comprehension and comprehension skills**: understanding what is being read is supported through a range of comprehension activities and frequent discussion opportunities.

- **Learning high frequency words**: *Letters and Sounds* high frequency words are carefully included within the **Project X CODE** books (called tricky words) and covered in the session notes.

- **Extending vocabulary**: vocabulary exploration is included and a careful selection of not yet decodable words appear in every second text. The session notes ensure children apply phonic knowledge and skills as their first approach to reading these words.

- **Ensuring motivation and engagement**: the gripping plot line, serial structure, familiar characters and innovative illustrations ensure readers become involved in the ongoing story right from the start.

- **Building reading stamina and reading fluency**: text length is increased in carefully controlled stages as **Project X CODE** progresses and a range of activities help to develop reading fluency.

- **Involving parents and carers**: opportunities to develop home-school links are provided, including advice on engaging parents/carers.

- **Tracking progress**: easy-to-use systems for tracking and assessing progress are built in at regular intervals, from each session to end of band checks.

- **Learning through a multi-sensory approach**: visual, auditory and kinaesthetic activities are included in **Project X CODE**.

Project X CODE structure chart

Book band Oxford Level	Zone	Book no.	Book title	Approximate reading age	Letters and Sounds Phase	NC levels
Yellow band Oxford Level 3	Bugtastic	1	The Web	Just 5 yrs	Phase 3 (including revision of Phase 2)	Low L1
		2	Cat's Quest			
		3	Missing!			
		4	BITE Fright			
	Galactic Orbit	5	Jet Attack			
		6	Return of the Jets			
		7	The Tower of Glass			
		8	Flight of Fear			
Blue band Oxford Level 4	Dragon Quest	9	Dragon Clash!	5–5.5 yrs	Phase 5 (including Phase 4 tricky words)	Secure L1
		10	The Hunt			
		11	Dragon Training			
		12	Into the Cave			
	Wild Rides	13	BITE Strike			
		14	Look Out!			
		15	The Thunderbolt			
		16	A Close Escape			
Green band Oxford Level 5	Jungle Trail	17	Stampede	5.5–6 yrs	Phase 5	High L1
		18	Scramble to Safety			
		19	Stuck!			
		20	Wild Rapids			
	Shark Dive	21	The Shark Sub			
		22	Underwater Chase			
		23	Sea Fright			
		24	All Tied Up			
Orange band Oxford Level 6	Fiendish Falls	25	Swoopie Mischief	6–6.5 yrs	Phase 5	Low L2
		26	Capsized!			
		27	The BITE Below			
		28	A Croco-BITE Smile			
	Big Freeze	29	Frozen with Fear			
		30	Snowball Attack			
		31	Skyway Shock			
		32	Ice Fight			
Turquoise band Oxford Level 7	Castle Kingdom	33	The Joust	6.5–7 yrs	Phase 5	Secure L2
		34	Locked Up!			
		35	Danger in the Tower			
		36	Battle for the Sword			
	Forbidden Valley	37	Up in the Air			
		38	Underground Escape			
		39	Volcano Blast			
		40	Dino Danger			
Purple band Oxford Level 8	Wonders of the World	41	Invisible Threat	7–7.5 yrs	Phase 5	High L2
		42	Statue Surprise			
		43	Scare in the Air			
		44	Secret of the Stone			
	Pyramid Peril	45	Into the Pyramid			
		46	Another Way In			
		47	Rock Shock			
		48	Hang On!			
Gold band Oxford Level 9	Marvel Towers	49	A Shock for Mini	7.5–8 yrs	Phase 5 (introducing Phase 6 suffixes)	Low L3
		50	A BITE Inside			
		51	Mission Marvel			
		52	Race Against Time			
	CODE Control	53	CODE's Countdown			
		54	The Last BITE			
		55	Eye to Eye			
		56	Stop CODE!			

Words using adjacent consonants, as taught in Phase 4, are used throughout as these provide excellent practice for blending.

Who Project X CODE is for

Project X CODE has been primarily designed as an intervention programme for children aged between 6 and 9 years old who are not meeting their expected reading levels. These children will already have been taught a full systematic synthetic phonics programme as part of their everyday learning but nevertheless demonstrate an insufficiently secure grasp of phonics and/or effective application in reading. They may also struggle with comprehension, motivation and oral vocabulary.

The **Project X CODE** approach is fully in line with the Phonics Screening Check to be undertaken by all children at the end of Year 1 in England, and the programme provides thorough revision and an incremental progression, which will support schools in ensuring that children's difficulties are addressed and that they are well prepared for retaking the test.

Project X CODE will be particularly effective in managing the transition between Years 2 and 3 (P3–4), especially for those children at risk of slipping back as a result of insecure attainment at the end of Year 2 (P3) and the six-week summer holiday.

Due to the high interest level of the books, children beyond 9 years of age may benefit from the programme. Schools could use the programme with older pupils, for example children with severe learning difficulties that present barriers to cognition and learning.

Characteristics of children who will benefit from Project X CODE

Children who will benefit from **Project X CODE** are likely to exhibit most or all of the following characteristics:

- Limited language experience, leading to limited vocabulary and poorly developed speaking and listening skills. They find it hard to respond to questions, engage in discussion or explain their reasoning/thought processes.
- Anxiety, frustration and lack of motivation. They may avoid reading, never choose to read voluntarily, or say things like, 'We haven't learned that yet', 'This is too hard for me' or even 'I can't read'.
- Dependency on adult support. They lack independent strategies to solve problems, so will often look to an adult to supply a word or tell them what to do.
- Difficulty with working memory. They are unable to retain, recall and rapidly retrieve relevant information.
- Problems with applying their learning in other contexts, e.g. they recognise many grapheme-phoneme correspondences (GPCs) but don't apply these in their reading.
- Spatial difficulties, e.g. left to right directionality and tracking a sentence from one line to the next.
- A need for over learning. They need to repeat the same strategy and practise the same skills many times more than their peers in order to commit these to memory and use them confidently.

The needs of different groups

Children who are falling behind with reading may also fall into one or more of the following groups.

Children identified as having Special Educational Needs (SEN)

Project X CODE may be very beneficial for children with a wide range of Special Educational Needs, irrespective of the stage at which they have been identified by the school. Schools will wish to consider the nature of the child's difficulties, the learning targets in place and who will deliver the individual or small group intervention sessions.

Children learning English as an Additional Language (EAL)

Project X CODE sessions are not suitable for children in the very early stages of English language acquisition but, especially where no other support is available, these children are likely to benefit from the programme once they are settled, have acquired a basic level of conversational English and have been taught a synthetic phonics programme. Where bilingual support teachers or teaching assistants are available, their involvement in **Project X CODE** will be invaluable.

Children with social, emotional and behavioural difficulties

Generally speaking, it is best to avoid including children with severe behavioural difficulties in **Project X CODE** small group sessions. However, a teaching assistant assigned to provide individual support to such a child could deliver the programme on an individual basis or work alongside another teaching assistant to include the child as part of the group.

Children with poor attendance

Evidence shows that inclusion in an intervention group, especially when the programme has a focus on motivation, as in **Project X CODE**, can act as an incentive to attend school more regularly and provide support to children who move between schools.

Project X CODE – At a glance

The launch story

Project X CODE builds excitement and interest from the start. Read the launch story, *The Adventure Begins*, and watch the animation before starting the programme (see page 53).

The Micro World poster

Create a stimulating intervention area, using this poster, where children can explore the wonders of Micro World as they progress through the books. They can also track their own progress by adding their names to character cards and moving these from zone to zone.

The reading books

Read the **Project X CODE** books in order to follow the exciting story and systematically build phonic and comprehension skills. There are two texts in each book – read one text in each 30-minute session.

The Teaching and Assessment Handbook

Each reading book is accompanied by carefully structured session notes and photocopiable resources (PCMs), including links to the classroom and home.

The handbook also includes a range of bespoke and easy-to-use tools to track children's progress at regular intervals (see page 24).

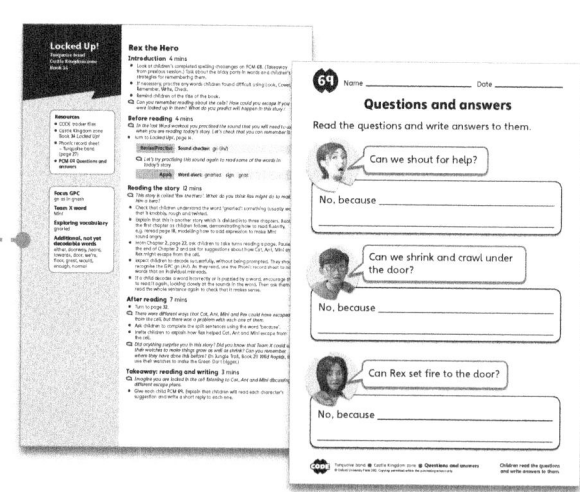

The Practice and Assessment CD-ROM

The *Practice and Assessment CD-ROM* provides a range of additional practice and assessment activities designed for independent use by children to help assess and track progress.

Once a child has completed the activities, a report is automatically generated, helping to pinpoint areas requiring further practice (see page 30).

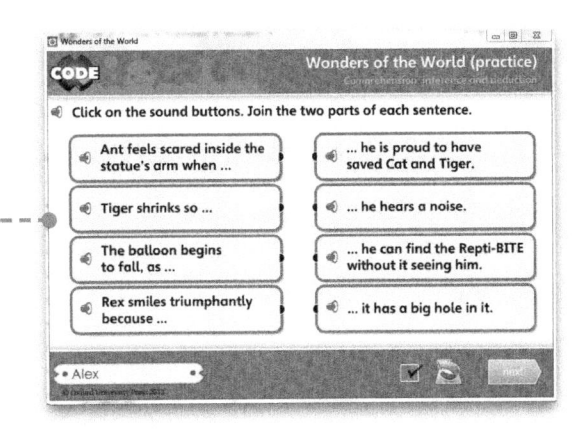

The eBooks

Project X CODE contains eBook versions of all the reading books, providing models of fluent, expressive reading, perfect for practice and consolidation when a child has read the print book. In addition, the eBooks can be used for small group teaching using an interactive whiteboard or computer.

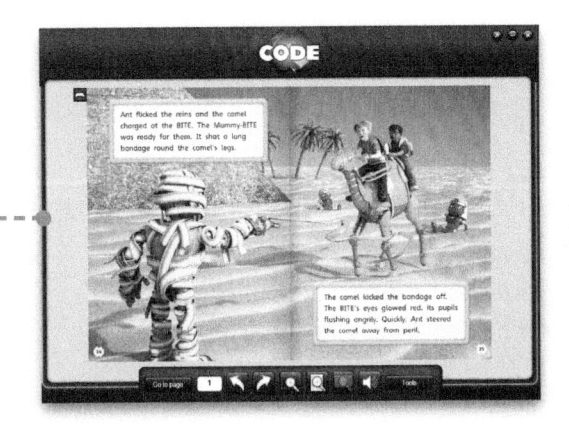

Professional Development

Project X CODE has been developed by a team of experts in phonics, intervention, reading engagement and comprehension (see page 8). They have created a series of short Professional Development film clips to support **Project X CODE** which are available on the *Practice and Assessment CD-ROM* and online at:
www.oxfordprimary.co.uk

Home-school links

Project X CODE supports the vital link between home and school through 'Takeaway' activities provided as part of the session notes in the handbook. In addition, a number of **Project X CODE** eBooks are available on Oxford Owl, our free website built to support parents with their child's learning.

Oxford OWL

For teachers
Helping you with free eBooks, inspirational resources, advice and support

For parents
Helping your child's learning with free eBooks, essential tips and fun activities

www.oxfordowl.co.uk

Project X CODE – A new approach

Project X CODE – The expert team

Project X CODE has been developed by leading experts in the fields of phonics, early intervention and comprehension to ensure **Project X CODE's** new approach provides maximum impact.

Marilyn Joyce

Marilyn is an expert in systematic synthetic phonics and early literacy development.

Di Hatchett

Di is an expert in early intervention in literacy and mathematics and the leadership of inclusion.

Maureen Lewis

Maureen is an expert in reading engagement and comprehension.

The reading books

Project X CODE is a book-by-book series to ensure the systematic development of synthetic phonics and comprehension skills. Each book in the series contains two texts.

> A book-by-book numbered adventure series.

Text 1: 100% decodable

Text 1 is short and fully decodable, containing the focus GPCs and tricky words (high frequency but not yet fully decodable words) which are practised before reading begins. Instantly applying this knowledge gives children a real sense of confidence.

> Children will identify with the popular characters and find the 3D look and feel engaging.

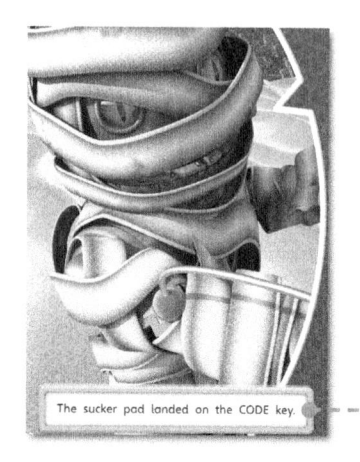

Text 2: at least 80% decodable

Text 2 is longer and includes the same focus GPCs and tricky words as Text 1. In addition, the text contains more varied vocabulary to create enthralling stories and develop comprehension skills at the right level of reading challenge.

> Dyslexia-friendly font

In-book support

Each book in the series contains in-book before and after reading pages, which are linked to the session notes and provide opportunities to focus on phonics and comprehension. The layout of these pages varies slightly through the book bands to increase the level of challenge as children's skills grow.

Before reading

These activities introduce the focus GPCs (suffixes at Gold), providing children with support to revise and practise specific phonic knowledge and skills, and to prepare to apply these to their reading of the text. They also encourage children to talk about the stories in preparation for reading.

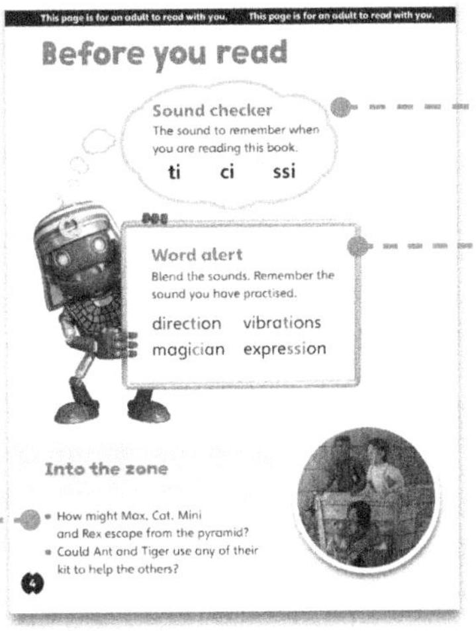

Into the zone creates opportunities for discussion, prediction and speculation about the story to come.

What does it mean? (Purple–Gold) provides opportunities to explore words children may find difficult before they encounter them in the text.

Sound checker (Yellow–Purple) introduces the GPCs that are covered in each text.

Sound spotter (Yellow–Turquoise)/Word alert (Turquoise–Gold) practises blending to encourage successful decoding. Some serve a double purpose: they illustrate the focus GPCs and introduce less familiar words, providing an opportunity to focus on both decoding and meaning at the same time. Sometimes practice GPCs are also covered.

After reading

These activities are designed to strengthen speaking and listening skills, and support children in building their vocabulary and comprehension skills. The activities focus on clarifying and deepening children's understanding of what they have just read. They also often contain a comment from one of the characters to encourage reflection and build engagement.

The in-book notes are for an adult to read and complete with a child, as indicated by the running banner at the top of each page.

Inside covers

Project X CODE books also include brief inside front cover notes for teachers/teaching assistants (full session notes are found in the **Project X CODE** *Teaching and Assessment Handbooks*).

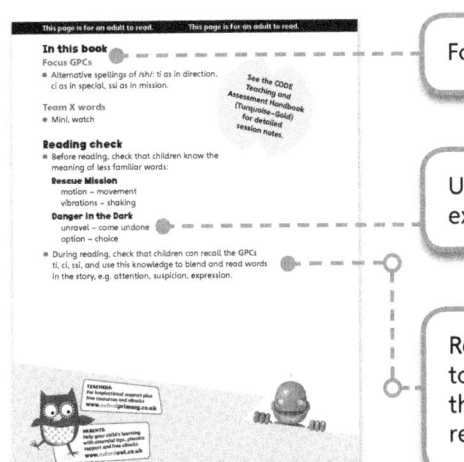

Focus GPCs are listed.

Useful vocabulary extension is provided.

Reminders are included to ensure children recall the focus GPCs during reading.

A new mission for Team X

The setting, characters and ongoing adventure in **Project X CODE** have been carefully designed to appeal to today's children, created specifically to hook children in from the start and keep them wanting to read on.

Micro World

The adventure stories are set in an amazing theme park, called Micro World, with 12 unique zones and two staff-only zones. In each zone there is a different setting and a fantastic ride, but what really makes Micro World different is that people have to shrink to get in.

Macro and Mini Marvel

Micro World was created by billionaire inventor Macro Marvel but it was actually his daughter, Mini Marvel's, idea. Macro Marvel wants to build a Micro World in every town and city.

Mini • Macro

CODE, MITEs and BITEs

Micro World is controlled by a central computer called **CODE** (**C**omputer **O**perated **D**igital **E**ntity). Day-to-day maintenance of the park is undertaken by small robots called MITEs and each zone is managed by a robot known as a BITE. The BITEs are different in each zone and, when they become angry, they develop powerful new capabilities.

CODE • A MITE • A BITE

The adventure begins

On opening day of Micro World, disaster strikes. As crowds gather to watch, Macro Marvel enters the Shrinker and disappears. CODE has gone wrong – it wants to keep people safe by shrinking the whole world. CODE believes this is the only way to conserve food resources and reduce pollution. Only one team can save the world now. It's time for Team X!

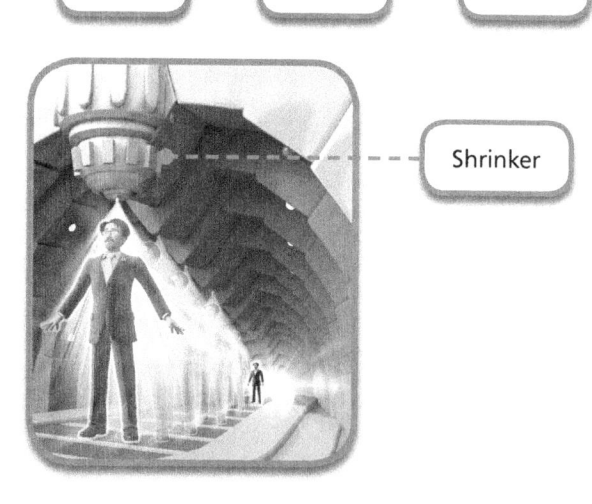

Shrinker

Team X

The exciting adventure stories in **Project X CODE** feature the popular Project X characters – Team X. Team X are four children with four amazing watches that allow them to shrink or grow to any size they want.

Max Cat Ant Tiger

Team X kit and craft

As well as amazing watches, Team X have special kit, such as a jet pack, bounce boots and power mitts, and craft such as the Grass Chopper, Driller and Hawkwing. Information about their watches, kit and craft can be found in the launch story, *The Adventure Begins* (pages 15–17).

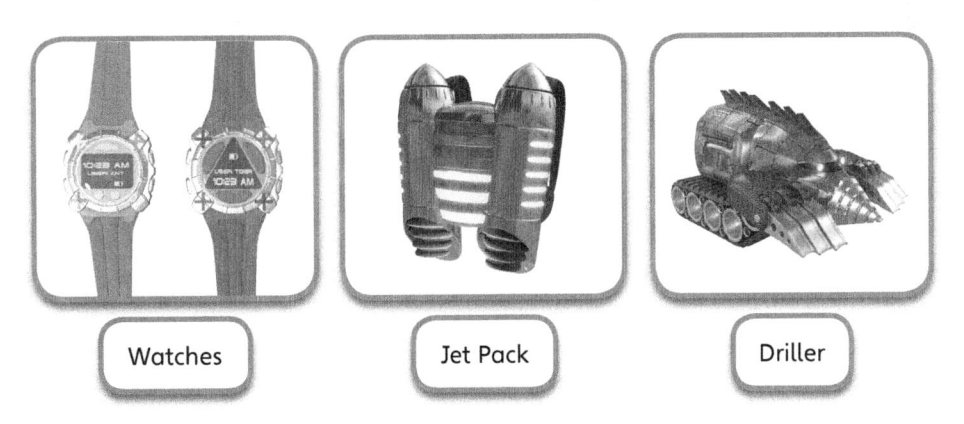

Watches Jet Pack Driller

The new mission

Team X fight to save the world from danger and they now have a new mission. Together, with Mini's help, they have to:

- Defeat the BITEs
- Collect the CODE keys
- Rescue Macro Marvel
- Stop CODE
- Save the world!

This story is told in full in *The Adventure Begins*, which can be found on the **Project X CODE** eBook CD-ROM, *Practice and Assessment CD-ROM* and online at www.oxfordprimary.co.uk

Project X CODE and your school's provision for intervention

Project X CODE is designed for use as soon as it is noted that children need additional support in order to keep up with their peers. It is also designed to fit into the layered approach to intervention used in the majority of schools, including a school's provision for Wave 3 support (children working either one-to-one or in very small groups) or Wave 2 support (children working in a group with a teaching assistant).

Wave 1	Quality first teaching	All children
Wave 2	Small group additional support	Just below average
Wave 3	Individual or very small group support with a trained teaching assistant	Struggling
Wave 3	Intensive support on an individual and/or very small group basis with a trained teacher	Lowest attaining

The programme design of **Project X CODE** enables flexible use by schools so that children can enter and exit the intervention at the appropriate level (7 entry points) or cluster of four books (14 entry points). (See page 23 for more information.)

Detailed session notes and easy-to-use systems to enable the tracking and assessment of progress are provided to support a trained teaching assistant in delivering rigorous and engaging sessions which will accelerate progress and develop children's confidence and independence as readers, either on a one-to-one basis or in small groups.

Project X CODE sessions have been designed so that they can be delivered to either individuals, pairs or to very small groups. The decision as to which is most appropriate needs to be made based on various factors which will be unique to every situation, bearing in mind both children's learning needs and the logistics of grouping and timetabling.

Individual sessions will have the advantage of providing a highly personalised approach and allow more time for a teacher or teaching assistant to focus on an individual's strengths, weaknesses and learning needs.

Paired or small group sessions will have the advantage that children are able to listen to, observe and learn from the contributions of others and to engage alongside peers in the discussion opportunities built into the sessions. They are also able to practise (in a supported situation) the all-important classroom skills of working both independently and co-operatively as part of a group.

Project X CODE also includes innovative materials designed to:

- ensure that the intervention sessions do not take place in isolation from the child's day-to-day experience of class teaching
- support the involvement of parents/carers and/or other adults who support the child's reading
- offer guidance (drawn from best practice in schools) for effective implementation and management in order to secure maximum impact on children's progress.

Phonic progression

Project X CODE provides the opportunity to revisit, practise and consolidate children's phonic skills and knowledge in a systematic and enjoyable way. Even if they have been taught a full synthetic phonic programme as part of their everyday learning, those identified for intervention may have an insufficient grasp of phonics as the prime approach.

For many children who struggle with phonics, the decoding process is slowed down to such an extent that pace and fluency of reading is affected and they may lose track of what they are reading. This often leads to frustration and a loss of motivation. **Project X CODE** is designed to strengthen children's ability to recognise GPCs rapidly and blend them effortlessly, thus developing automaticity in decoding whilst also practising high frequency tricky words such as *was*, *come*, *your* and *there* which are fundamental to fluency. As the programme progresses, segmentation for spelling is also introduced.

Project X CODE and *Letters and Sounds*

Project X CODE follows the phonic progression used in *Letters and Sounds* and other high-quality phonic programmes, incorporating the high frequency tricky words. An integral spiral structure constantly revises prior learning whilst revisiting each group of GPCs from Phase 3 to Phase 5 and beyond.

The first band of books (Yellow band) explicitly covers Phase 3 but also reinforces Phase 2. Words, including adjacent consonants, which are taught separately in Phase 4, are used throughout the series as experience shows that children do not find them problematic and they provide excellent practice in blending.

The new and alternative graphemes and pronunciations represented by *Letters and Sounds* Phase 5, which often present a stumbling block to children at risk of reading failure, are spread across six bands of books (Blue to Gold bands), to allow for plenty of practice and consolidation. The spiral approach includes some alternative graphemes/spellings for phonemes, ensuring that when children encounter additional alternative graphemes, they also revisit the ones they already know.

The stories in Project X CODE and decodability

Amongst the research evidence supporting the use of decodable books with beginner readers, Vadasy's 2005 research paper[1] observed:

Text considerations like decodability appear to be more important for less skilled students who require more scaffolded literacy experiences.

Each **Project X CODE** book includes two texts that drive forward the Micro World adventure. The fully decodable first text gives each child the optimum ingredients for reading success, which serves to affirm the child's success and whets their appetite for further challenge.

The longer second text creates more enthralling stories using more varied vocabulary, providing a rich context to develop comprehension – often an area of difficulty for struggling readers. Tackling this vocabulary will support the children to make more rapid progress in pace, fluency and understanding.

Project X CODE – Phonic progression chart

Band	Book	Title	Grapheme						Phoneme	Practice GPCs				Tricky words			
Yellow	1	The Web	j	v	w	z	zz		/j/ /v/ /w/ /z/	s /s/			ss /s/	he	she	they	are
	2	Cat's Quest	x	y	qu				/x/ /y/ /qu/					was	you	my	
	3	Missing!	ch	th	sh	ng			/ch/ /th/ /sh/ /ng/					me	we	be	
	4	BITE Fright	ai	ee	igh				/ai/ /ee/ /igh/					her	all		
	5	Jet Attack	oa						/oa/								
	6	Return of the Jets		oo					/oo/ short and long					Phase 3 tricky words are repeated.			
	7	The Tower of Glass	ar	or	ur	ow			/ar/ /or/ /ur/ /er/								
	8	Flight of Fear			oi				/oi/								
Blue			air	ure	ear				/air/ /ure/ /ear/								
	9	Dragon Clash!			ed				/d/ /t/					said	like	what	
	10	The Hunt			wh				/w/	w /w/				so	have	were	there
	11	Dragon Training			y				/ee/	y /y/	ee /ee/			some	come	do	
					oy				/oi/	oi /oi/	a e i o u short vowels practice						
					ou				/ou/	ow /ou/							
	12	Into the Cave	a	a-e	ay				/ai/		ai /ai/			little	one	your	
	13	BITE Strike	i	i-e					/igh/		igh /igh/						
	14	Look Out!		e-e	ea				/ee/	ee /ee/	y /ee/						
	15	The Thunderbolt	o	o-e					/oa/		oa /oa/			Phase 4 tricky words are repeated.			
	16	A Close Escape	u	u-e					long /oo/, /(y)oo/		Practise and consolidate all split digraphs.						
Green	17	Stampede			le				/ul/		l /l/			who	where	any	
	18	Scramble to Safety	ie		ph				/f/	f /f/				who	where	any	
					y				/igh/	igh /igh/	i-e /igh/						
					oe				/oa/	o /oa/	o-e /oa/						
	19	Stuck!			ue				/(y)oo/ and long /oo/		ue /(y)oo/	u-e long /oo/		oh	many	work	
	20	Wild Rapids			ea				/ee/	ee /ee/	y /ee/ e-e /ee/			oh	many	water	
	21	The Shark Sub			ea				/e/		e /e/			because	people	water	
	22	Underwater Chase			ir				/ur/	ur /ur/		oo short and long /oo/		because	water	work	
			ew		ou												
Orange	23	Sea Fright			se				/s/	s /s/				laughed	different		
									/z/	z /z/	zz /z/						
	24	All Tied Up	aw		au				/or/		or /or/			called	friend		
	25	Swoopie Mischief			ie				/ee/		ie /igh/			called	friend		
					s				/zh/								
	26	Capsized!			tch				/ch/	ch /ch/	sh /sh/						
					ture				/ch/								
	27	The BITE Below	ow	ough	ou				/oa/		oa /oa/			thought	friend		
	28	A Croco-BITE Smile	o	oo	ou				/u/		u /u/			thought	through		

Band	Book	Title	Grapheme				Phoneme	Practice GPCs				Tricky words			
												once	eyes	through	eyes
Orange	29	Frozen with Fear	ce			sc	/s/	se /s/	s /s/	ss /s/				their	
	30	Snowball Attack		c (soft)			/s/	th /th/					their			once
	31	Skyway Shock	ge			dge	/j/	j /j/								
	32	Ice Fight		g (soft)			/j/									
	33	The Joust			ey		/ee/	y /ee/		ng /ng/						
	34	Locked Up!			kn		/n/			n /n/						
	35	Danger in the Tower	a		gn		/n/									
Turquoise	36	Battle for the Sword	a		al		/ar/	•		ar /ar/						
					sw		/s/	s /s/								
					st		/s/									
					ve		/v/			v /v/						
	37	Up in the Air	oor	ore	our	oar	/or/	or /or/								
	38	Underground Escape	ough	augh	al		/or/	or /or/	aw /or/	au /or/						
	39	Volcano Blast	Schwa vowel sounds*				/ə/		er							
	40	Dino Danger	ear	(w)or			/ur/		ir /ur/							
	41	Invisible Threat	eer	ere	ier		/eer/	ear /eer/		air /air/						
	42	Statue Surprise		gh	gu		/g/	g /g/	m /m/	mm /m/						
					mb		/m/									
					s		silent									
	43	Scare in the Air			gh		/f/	ph /f/	f /f/	ff /f/						
			are	ear	ere		/air/									
Purple	44	Secret of the Stone	ei	eigh	aigh	ey	/ai/	ay /ai/	ai /ai/	a /ai/	a-e /ai/					
	45	Into the Pyramid			ch		/sh/									
					ch		/k/									
					y		/i/									
	46	Another Way In	ti	ci	ssi		/sh/	sh /sh/	ch /ch/	ch /sh/						
	47	Rock Shock			si		/zh/			s /zh/						
	48	Hang On!	el	il	al		/ul/			le /ul/						
	49	A Shock for Mini			oul		short /oo/	oo long /oo/	ue long /oo/ and /(y)oo/	u-e long /oo/	ew long /oo/	o /oa/					
Gold	50	A BITE Inside	wr		rh		/r/	r /r/		rr /rr/						
	51	Mission Marvel			wh		/h/			h /h/						
				(w)ar	(w)a		/or/									
				a(lt)	(w)a		/ol/									
		Suffixes														
	52	Race Against Time	-s	-es	-ies			s /s/	s /z/	ie /ee/						
	53	CODE's Countdown			-ed					ed /d/, /t/						
	54	The Last BITE			-ing					ng /ng/						
	55	Eye to Eye	-y		-ly					y /ee/						
	56	Stop CODE!														

*Schwa is the name for the most common sound in English. It is a weak, unstressed sound that occurs in many words, e.g motor, cupboard, possible.
Note: Words using adjacent consonants, as taught in Phase 4, are used throughout as these provide excellent practice for blending.

Tricky words from the previous phases are repeated.

Comprehension progression

Project X CODE is a balanced intervention programme which, from the earliest stage, supports reading comprehension as well as a 'phonics first' approach. Most adults who listen to children read will have experienced times when the child's comments or responses to questions and discussion show that they have very little understanding of what they have just read, even though they have decoded it successfully. It is critical to develop children's reading skills to help them understand that texts carry meaningful messages and to support them in exploring those meanings.

For teaching purposes it is useful to separate the processes of decoding and comprehension and recognise that the balance of effort given to either of these processes will shift within texts and over time. As children acquire an increasing repertoire of known words and can effectively apply their phonic knowledge to new words, less time is given to the decoding process.

Comprehension within Project X CODE

Comprehension within **Project X CODE** follows a progression which will be familiar to schools; it moves children from simple literal aspects of comprehension (e.g. locating information in the texts) and simple inference (e.g. making links between information in the texts and personal experience) to more demanding application of these skills. Other aspects of comprehension (e.g. empathy and summary) are developed in the same way.

As the comprehension process and skills used to understand a text are the same whatever the age or ability of the reader, progression in **Project X CODE** is achieved through differentiating the level of support the reader needs, the types of activity they are asked to do and the complexity of the text they are asked to deal with. Within **Project X CODE**, activities progress from simple, supported tasks to increasingly demanding, independent tasks, e.g. simple sequencing using picture prompts progresses to oral story summary without prompts.

Extending and exploring vocabulary

Another critical element of learning to read is extending children's vocabulary and exploring the meanings of words. Such explorations clear up any misunderstandings caused by not knowing what a word means. However, the relationship between reading and vocabulary goes beyond just knowing what individual words mean. Most new vocabulary is acquired via reading once we have a core of oral everyday words. Children with poor oral vocabulary often struggle to learn to read and children who don't read often have a limited vocabulary.

Extending children's oral vocabulary and personal 'store' of vocabulary has a beneficial impact on reading so every **Project X CODE** session contains a dedicated 'Exploring vocabulary/What does it mean?' section, and every Text 2 in the books includes a range of not yet decodable words.

> **Tip**
> Text 2 in each book contains some words that are not yet fully decodable (detailed in the session notes), although children may be familiar with them. If a child struggles to read one of these words, encourage them to sound out as much of the word as they can. Then tell them the word and get them to repeat it. Do not encourage them to guess the word.

Project X CODE – Comprehension progression chart

	Describe, select or retrieve information, events or ideas from texts Use evidence from text	Understand, deduce, infer or interpret information, events or ideas from texts	Understand vocabulary Explain and comment on writers' use of language Understand textual differences
Comprehension skills developed across Project X CODE	• Recall • Retrieval • Sequencing • Summarising • Visualisation and other sensory responses	• Prediction • Linking text to prior knowledge • Synthesising information from different parts of the text • Empathy • Visualisation and other sensory responses • Inference and deduction	• Vocabulary exploration • Recognition and understanding of literary devices • Understanding of different text types and their characteristics
Before reading activities	• Examination of cover/title to retrieve information • Oral recall of previous story/story so far	• Examination of 'Into the zone' questions • Recall of previous events to encourage prediction • Speculation on how characters might be feeling	• Exploring meaning of vocabulary likely to cause difficulties • Words/phrases to look out for while reading
During reading activities	modelled by adult ⟶ prompted by adult ⟶ used independently • Check meaning of unknown words • Reread a sentence or paragraph to give it more conscious attention • Temporarily tolerate some ambiguity/lack of understanding and after decoding read on to see if the sense becomes clearer as more information is revealed • Share any lack of understanding with someone else and discuss what it means together		
After reading activities	• Oral questions and discussion • 'Show me the page where …' • Scanning text for evidence • 'Ask me about' labels • Story sequencing/retelling • Adding captions • Cloze sentences • 'Say, think, feel' activities • Five senses activities	• Oral questions and discussion • 'Ask me about' labels • 'Say, think, feel' activities • Five senses activities • 1 + 1 = 2: Synthesising (i.e. 1 fact + 1 fact gives a new fact) • Character profiles • Cause and effect: 'Why did that happen?' • Alternative viewpoint: retelling a story from the point of view of another character • Shrink the story: summarise chapters	• Oral questions and discussion • Finding themed words, e.g. sounds • Word temperature activities (identifying words of increasing intensity) • Recognise and use different genres, e.g. explanation, instruction • Why did the author choose that? Focusing on words, phrases, similes, etc. • Practising fluent, expressive reading, taking account of punctuation • Spelling activities • Alternative viewpoint: taking a critical stance

A summary of progression

The phonics and comprehension demands within the books and the level of challenge in the sessions develop as the programme progresses. The language of the reading prompts and feedback similarly develop to match the progress achieved by the child. This ensures that the child encounters the appropriate level of challenge and support at every stage.

Phonic progression by band

Yellow and Blue bands

- Oral blending and segmentation
- Recall of GPCs
- Blending and segmentation activities
- Manipulating phonemes

Green and Orange bands

- Recall of GPCs
- Introduction of 'spelling' in terms of writing graphemes
- Text 1: reading words, new phonemes and variants
- Text 2: revision of new GPCs, focus on tricky words

Turquoise and Purple bands

- Text 1: preceded by a Word workout which reminds children of the focus GPC, it is to be treated as a 'quick read'. The decoding practice called upon in Text 1 is treated as a 'warm up' for Text 2
- Text 2: a 'phonics workout' in terms of applying concepts whilst reading 'on the run'
- Greater challenge and content in 'Takeaway' activities

Gold band

- As Turquoise and Purple bands above
- Guided reading introduced rather than reading in turn
- Focus shifts to fluency and reading stamina

Comprehension progression by band

Yellow to Gold bands

These comprehension skills are used in all bands but the degree of challenge increases:
- prediction
- recall
- inference and deduction
- information retrieval
- sequencing
- summarising
- synthesising information from different parts of the text
- empathy
- visualisation and other sensory responses
- taking a critical stance

Reading enrichment

Project X CODE is specifically designed to address key areas shown by research to be important in developing sustained interest in reading as a rewarding and informative experience.

Ensuring and maintaining motivation and engagement

Because of their disheartening early experiences, struggling readers often have little self-motivation to read. They can also have negative attitudes towards reading. However, as the reading process begins to make more sense to them, struggling readers usually begin to experience increased success and reward from their reading.

Project X CODE helps build children's enthusiasm for reading by:

- offering opportunities for struggling readers to share the pleasures of reading through hearing fluent reading via the eBooks
- using texts with familiar characters, exciting contexts and an ongoing adventure with regular cliffhangers to keep children 'hooked' and eager to find out what happens next
- ensuring appropriate challenge so that reading sessions do not reinforce failure – the materials are matched to children's needs by carefully structured progression through the levels
- creating times to read and discuss texts with others – children need to experience reading as a social, collaborative event, not just as an individual endeavour
- giving children feedback on their achievement as they are reading
- recognising and celebrating progress over time by showing progress in concrete ways, e.g. tracking children's progress through the zones, using external motivators such as certificates to help motivate children for the 'long haul'
- developing home-school partnerships to support children
- building automaticity in decoding so that it requires less effort, freeing children to focus on comprehension.

Helping children face reading challenges

For some children, progress may continue to feel effortful and even successful learners may find themselves struggling over specific aspects of learning which they find more challenging.

It is important to look out for times when learning might prove challenging for specific children (including in-class times when their lack of parity with peers may be evident). Careful tracking of progress will help identify when a child is at risk of struggling and action can rapidly be taken, such as:

- **Extra practice**: offer additional support for specific problem areas by providing focused games and activities, revisiting phonic activities from earlier levels (see pages 47–49 for activities), using the *Practice and Assessment CD-ROMs*, or reading further books that practise the GPCs.
- **In-class support**: provide support in whole-class learning through careful grouping, support from well trained and briefed additional adults, and carefully differentiated materials and tasks.
- **Overlearning**: provide opportunities to 'overlearn' by working at the same level for an additional period of time, until the learning is secure.
- **'Easy' reading**: rebuild reading confidence by providing opportunities for some 'easy' reading, i.e. books pitched at a level below the present challenge level, whilst also moving forward with new learning.
- **Expert roles**: create opportunities for children to take on 'expert' roles by updating the class about the **Project X CODE** adventures and being a **Project X CODE** ambassador for children new to **Project X CODE**.

Building self-confidence

Many struggling readers suffer from a lack of self-confidence. This has a detrimental effect on their learning by making them reluctant to risk failure and thus inhibiting their willingness to 'have a go'. Counteracting this lack of confidence and developing self-esteem are important steps to developing children as independent learners. Some strategies that might help include:

- **The language of success**: counteract children's negative feelings by using positive language, e.g. *Do you remember when we practised X and you got it all right?* or *Yes, you did get a bit muddled here but let's look at what you got right and that will help with the bits that caused a problem.*
- **Characteristics of successful learners**: discuss and support the development of successful learner characteristics by helping children:
  - recognise negative feelings and how to overcome them
  - acknowledge their self-agency in achieving goals
  - develop emotional persistence and resilience to achieve goals.
- **Thought showering**: discuss ideas to overcome learning problems, e.g. what to do when they get stuck, don't know the answer, etc.
- **Prompt cards**: create cards to remind children of strategies they can use.
- **Role play**: act out how to respond to specific problems, e.g. *He said I'm dumb 'cos I can't read.*
- **Learning stories**: use 'learning stories' to prompt reflection and discussion. These can be linked to the curriculum.
- **Praise circles**: encourage children to say something positive about the skills of the child sitting next to them.
- **Praise silhouettes**: encourage teachers, teaching assistants and children to record positive comments about a child and their learning in a silhouette of them.

Moving to independence

Project X CODE is carefully structured to move readers from the early stages of learning to read to a point at which they have caught up with age-related expectations. As they progress through **Project X CODE** the level of challenge is increased in the following ways to ensure children develop the skills and confidence of an independent reader while maintaining motivation.

Language complexity

Project X CODE develops language complexity in Turquoise to Gold bands by:

- increasing the length of sentences, and the complexity of sentence structures and vocabulary
- introducing speech and paragraph breaks.

The more complex written language scaffolds children's own increasing capability in both spoken and written language and helps develop independence by providing models of what they already know but also introducing new structures such as increased use of clauses.

Developing storylines

The greater length and more sophisticated language structures in the Turquoise to Gold bands of **Project X CODE** allow for more complex storylines and characterisation. These help maintain motivation and give exciting opportunities for children to experience the pleasures of reading – important elements in developing independent, lifelong readers who choose to read.

Reading fluency

Project X CODE incorporates repetition of words, opportunities to reread texts and vocabulary-building activities – all important for developing fluency, which makes independent reading a more rewarding experience. The more complex language structures and dialogue develop children's reading fluency by providing models of natural language. Fluency is further supported with eBooks, enabling children to listen to/read along with an expert reader. There are opportunities in the sessions to read aloud and listen to fluent reading.

Reading stamina

As children become more skilled at automatic decoding and their bank of known words grows, their reading pace increases and they can read more within a session. By the Purple and Gold bands, children are reading short chapter books, practising their growing reading skills and starting to see themselves as successful readers. The introduction of guided reading at Gold band gives children even more opportunity for individual, independent reading.

> **Tip**
>
> ### Developing as a reader
>
> As well as scaffolding towards independent reading, children also need opportunities to apply their reading skills more widely and develop their own reading tastes. Provide opportunities beyond the **Project X CODE** sessions for independent reading using both known and new texts. Children should be encouraged to choose from a wide range of books, including non-fiction texts.

Learning to spell with Project X CODE

A key principle of all high-quality phonic programmes is that decoding (responding to letters by pronouncing and blending individual phonemes into whole words) and encoding (segmenting whole spoken words into individual phonemes and selecting letters to represent those phonemes) are reversible processes. Thus children learn to use letters to represent phonemes and this is the foundation of spelling.

Teaching segmentation for spelling involves a combination of oral segmentation of a word and letter recall in terms of the graphemes which represent the phonemes. It is recognised as usually lagging behind proficiency in blending for reading. This is because spelling generally requires the recalling and composing of a word from memory. Struggling readers frequently have problems with working memory (the retention and recall of information 'on the run').

Children face an additional challenge when reading and spelling become less easily reversible, as in *Letters and Sounds* Phase 5, when words contain sounds (particularly vowel sounds) that can be spelled in more than one way, e.g. /ai/ can be spelled a, a-e, ay, ai, ei, eigh, aigh, -ey.

Project X CODE builds in intensive practice and repetition opportunities to help develop working memory and helps children begin to learn and practise the vital skill of spelling in the following ways:

- **Recognising phonemes**: from the earliest levels, **Project X CODE** involves children in activities requiring the recognising and transcribing of graphemes when given a sound. The **Phoneme count** activity (page 48) involves children in counting phonemes in words spoken aloud (without the printed version available) – a key skill for developing accurate spelling.

- **Segmenting for spelling**: the **Quickwrite** activity (page 48) is directly related to segmentation as the children are involved in listening to a particular word being spoken aloud, repeating it and saying the individual phonemes to themselves, then writing the word on their whiteboards.

- **Alternative spellings**: considerable attention is paid in **Project X CODE** sessions to the particularly challenging area of alternative pronunciation and spellings of phonemes. At the higher levels, children have opportunities to use the well-known 'Look, Cover, Remember, Write, Check' process for practising/memorising spellings, introduced at Green band and continued through to Gold band.

The selection process for Project X CODE

The selection process for **Project X CODE** should be informed by your school's own records of progress in reading, phonic assessments and general tracking procedures for children identified as at risk of falling behind age-related expectations.

Entry criteria

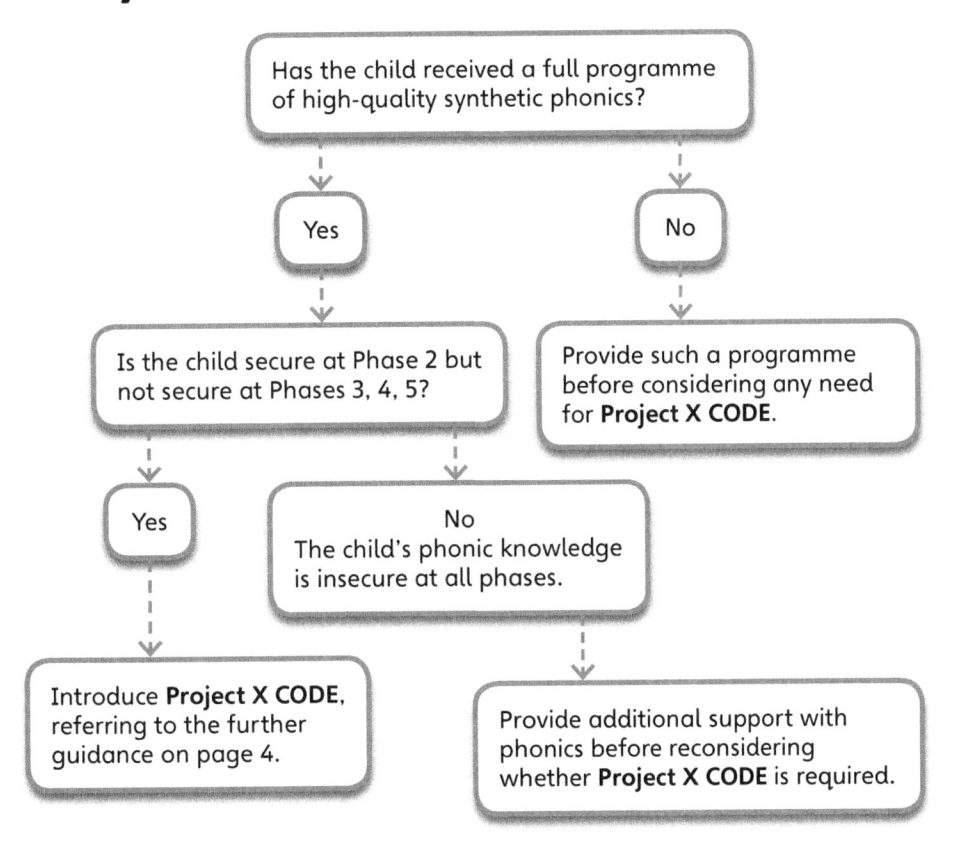

```
        Has the child received a full programme
          of high-quality synthetic phonics?
                    /              \
                  Yes               No
                   |                 |
    Is the child secure at     Provide such a programme
    Phase 2 but not secure     before considering any need
    at Phases 3, 4, 5?         for Project X CODE.
        /         \
      Yes          No
                   The child's phonic knowledge
                   is insecure at all phases.
       |                        |
  Introduce Project X CODE,   Provide additional support with
  referring to the further    phonics before reconsidering
  guidance on page 4.         whether Project X CODE is required.
```

Choosing the right level

Once children have been selected to use **Project X CODE**, the level at which they should enter the programme needs to be determined. A number of the **Project X CODE** assessment resources can be used to help select the appropriate level or cluster of books for each child:

- **Phonic progression chart** (pages 14–15): indicates the GPCs covered in each book and can be used to assess which phonemes are problematic for each child.
- **End of band progress checks** (pages 33–35): can offer guidance as to the skills children should be secure in at the end of each level. (Please note – book-specific references are not applicable as an entry level assessment.)
- **End of band reading passages** (pages 39–41): can be used to check the level at which children are reading comfortably.
- **Pseudo words**: can be found in the last book in each cluster of four books. These can be used to see how well children phonically decode and blend the GPCs in each cluster.

Tracking and assessing progress

Tracking and assessing progress at regular intervals is crucial for assessing the impact of any intervention. **Project X CODE** includes a range of bespoke and easy-to-use tools which support both day-to-day and summative assessment. The purpose of these tools is to enable quick and easy assessment to gauge how well the intervention is working for each child and whether there are specific areas which need follow-up action as part of class work.

Tools for assessing progress

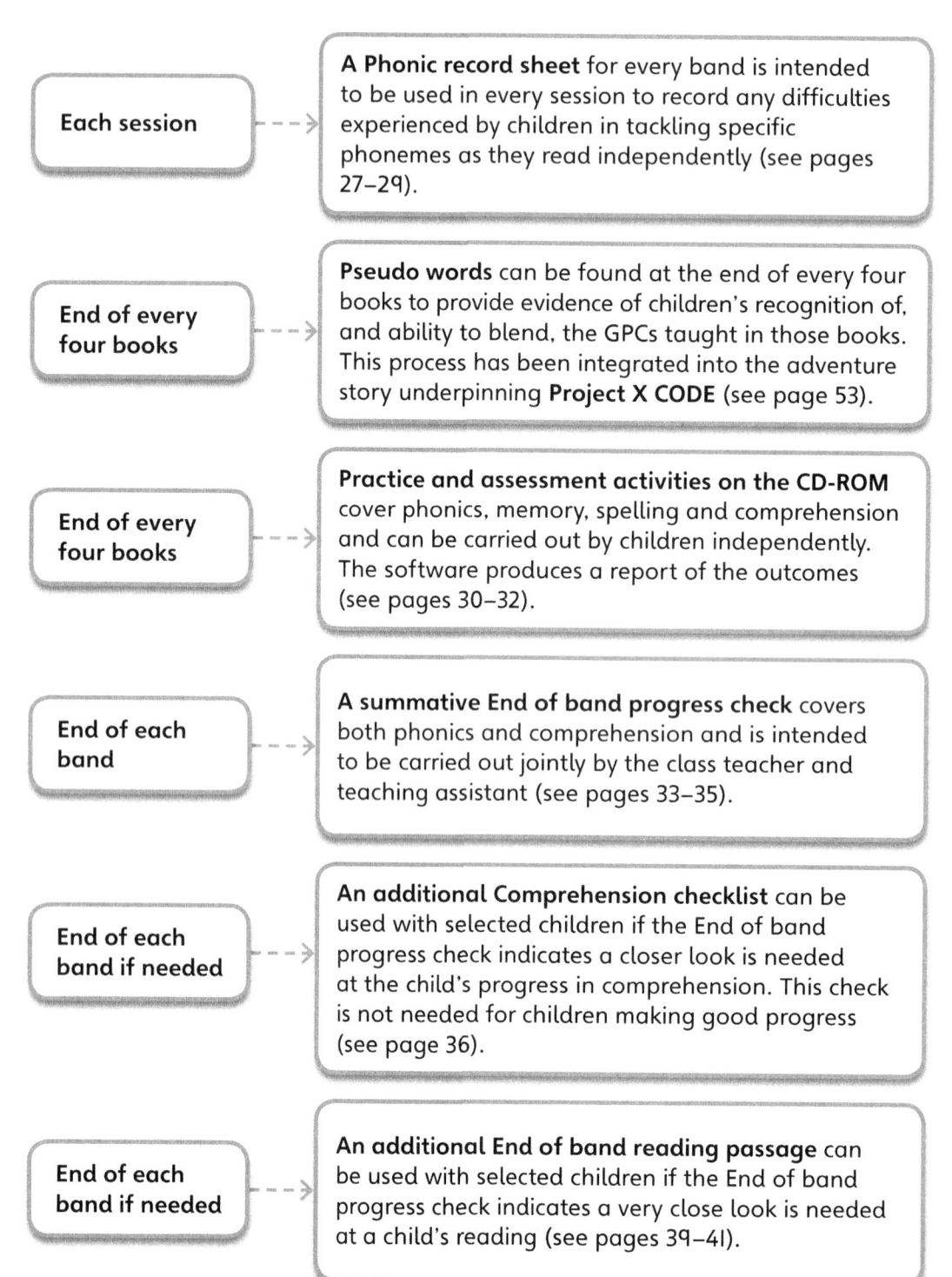

Each session ⇢ **A Phonic record sheet** for every band is intended to be used in every session to record any difficulties experienced by children in tackling specific phonemes as they read independently (see pages 27–29).

End of every four books ⇢ **Pseudo words** can be found at the end of every four books to provide evidence of children's recognition of, and ability to blend, the GPCs taught in those books. This process has been integrated into the adventure story underpinning **Project X CODE** (see page 53).

End of every four books ⇢ **Practice and assessment activities on the CD-ROM** cover phonics, memory, spelling and comprehension and can be carried out by children independently. The software produces a report of the outcomes (see pages 30–32).

End of each band ⇢ A summative **End of band progress check** covers both phonics and comprehension and is intended to be carried out jointly by the class teacher and teaching assistant (see pages 33–35).

End of each band if needed ⇢ An additional **Comprehension checklist** can be used with selected children if the End of band progress check indicates a closer look is needed at the child's progress in comprehension. This check is not needed for children making good progress (see page 36).

End of each band if needed ⇢ An additional **End of band reading passage** can be used with selected children if the End of band progress check indicates a very close look is needed at a child's reading (see pages 39–41).

Following up on assessment findings

Phonic record sheet

This is a quick and easy way to note any GPCs which cause a child problems with decoding. These GPCs should be revisited by returning to the problematic word and supporting the child to try reading it again. If the problem persists:

- help the child recall the sound made by the relevant letter(s) and then have another go at decoding the word
- look out for this phoneme in future texts and repeat the follow-up if the child falters again. If they are successful, take them back to look at the relevant word and give specific praise
- provide the child with additional opportunities (in class independent working time) for practising phoneme recognition using games (see pages 47–49) or the **Project X CODE** *Practice and Assessment CD-ROM*, if there is a continuing issue with a particular phoneme.

Pseudo words

These are designed to check whether the child can recognise and blend the GPCs taught in each cluster of four books. When working through these words, any phonically viable answer should be counted as correct, regardless of pronunciation, e.g. 'yoot' pronounced the same way as 'foot' or 'hoot'. If a particular phoneme/group of phonemes is causing a problem, provide the child with additional opportunities to practise the phonemes as described above.

End of band progress checks

These are intended to give a rounded picture of the child's progress. If the child is **achieving the majority of objectives**, there is no need for further action and the child should continue with **Project X CODE** until they have caught up with their peers and can exit the programme.

If a child is **not achieving the majority of objectives**, follow-up actions should be taken, for example, using the additional End of band reading passages and/or the additional Comprehension checklist to analyse areas of specific difficulty.

Serious consideration should be given to the reasons underlying the child's difficulties. It may be that the child was not sufficiently secure with core phonic knowledge and therefore needs some intensive support or further specialist investigation.

If the End of band progress check shows that the child is **making good progress, but that some areas are causing concern**, opportunities should be provided for in-class follow-up while the child continues on to the next stage of **Project X CODE**. Such opportunities might include:

- using games (see pages 47–49) or the *Practice and Assessment CD-ROM* to practise phoneme recognition
- using comprehension activities (see pages 51–52) as part of group work or the *Practice and Assessment CD-ROM*
- implementing additional or targeted guided reading sessions
- encouraging independent reading using texts previously covered in **Project X CODE** sessions
- working with an adult, using the before and after reading pages in familiar **Project X CODE** books, listening to the **Project X CODE** eBooks and 'reading along' in order to practise fluency and expression.

Determining when to leave Project X CODE

Project X CODE has been carefully designed for flexible use by schools in terms of entry and exit levels. The point at which a child is ready to leave **Project X CODE** depends on the aims of the intervention and the needs of the learner – a child may be ready to leave the programme after reading a cluster of books, a book band or after completing the whole programme.

The ongoing tracking and assessment built into **Project X CODE**, along with teacher and teaching assistant discussions, will enable informed decisions to be made about the best point for children to leave **Project X CODE**.

Securing and maintaining gains after Project X CODE

Once children complete any additional intervention programme such as **Project X CODE**, it is vital that their progress is monitored and checked regularly in order to ensure that the gains made are not lost. To help with this, establish the following:

- **Evaluation**: both immediate and longer term evaluation of the impact of interventions used in the school are incorporated into the school self-evaluation process.
- **Tracking**: children are flagged on the school's tracking system so that all class teachers are aware that they require additional support in order to keep up with their peers and may need further support in the future.
- **Support**: teaching assistants who support the children are well trained, have access to regular updating of their skills and are entitled to quality assurance and clear management in the same way as other staff.
- **Ability groups**: children's placement in class ability groups is regularly reviewed, particularly when a child has made significant progress as part of an intervention programme, to ensure they are always working at the right level.
- **Group work**: the effectiveness of guided group work is focused on as part of evaluation of class teaching, particularly assessing the impact on children at risk of underachievement.
- **Ongoing assessment**: the **Project X CODE** assessment materials are used alongside the school's own tracking systems to check progress regularly, both during and following their intervention programme.
- **Home-school links**: continue to work closely with parents and carers to ensure the child's learning at home is sustained and tailored to the family context. (See the **Project X CODE** *Practice and Assessment CD-ROM* for editable parent/carer resources.)
- **Homework help**: give children who do not receive help at home access to 'homework' activities or 'buddy reading' with someone who has been trained as a reading partner, for example a teaching assistant, older primary child, secondary school pupil or an adult volunteer.

> **Tip**
>
> **More help needed?**
>
> Many children who have struggled to become fluent readers may continue to encounter stumbling blocks after they have successfully completed an intervention. It is important that their progress is carefully tracked and prompt action taken if they show signs of being at risk of falling behind again. Preventative action such as very short periods of further support closely tailored to the individual's needs and the learning area causing difficulty is likely to help avoid the need for another intensive period of additional support.

Project X CODE Phonic record sheet – Turquoise band (Castle Kingdom and Forbidden Valley)

As the children read, record any words they misread in the relevant box. The focus GPCs for each book are listed, enabling you to identify any particular GPCs that are proving problematic and need further consolidation.

Editable version available on the Project X CODE Practice and Assessment CD-ROM

	Castle Kingdom				Forbidden Valley			
Name of child	The Joust ey kn /n/	Locked Up! gn /n/	Danger in the Tower al /ar/ a /ar/ sw /s/	Battle for the Sword st /s/ ve /v/	Up in the Air oor ore our /or/ oar	Underground Escape ough /or/ augh /or/ al /or/	Volcano Blast ('schwa') re /uh/ our /uh/	Dino Danger ear /ur/ (w)or /ur/

Turquoise band ● Castle Kingdom and Forbidden Valley ● **Phonic record sheet**

© Oxford University Press 2012. Copying permitted within the purchasing school only.

Project X CODE Phonic record sheet – Purple band (Wonders of the World and Pyramid Peril)

As the children read, record any words they misread in the relevant box. The focus GPCs for each book are listed, enabling you to identify any particular GPCs that are proving problematic and need further consolidation.

Editable version available on the Project X CODE Practice and Assessment CD-ROM

Name of child	Wonders of the World					Pyramid Peril			
	Invisible Threat eer ere /eer/ ier /eer/	Statue Surprise gh /g/ gu /g/ mb /m/ (silent) s	Scare in the Air gh /f/ are /air/ ear /air/ ere /air/	Secret of the Stone ei /ai/ eigh /ai/ aigh /ai/ ey /ai/	Into the Pyramid ch /sh/ ch /k/ y /i/	Another Way In ti /sh/ ci /sh/ ssi /sh/	Rock Shock si /zh/	Hang On! el /ul/ il /ul/ al /ul/	

Purple band ● Wonders of the World and Pyramid Peril ●
Phonic record sheet

© Oxford University Press 2012. Copying permitted within the purchasing school only.

Project X CODE Phonic record sheet – Gold band (Marvel Towers and CODE Control)

Editable version available on the Project X CODE Practice and Assessment CD-ROM

As the children read, record any words they misread in the relevant box. The focus GPCs for each book are listed, enabling you to identify any particular GPCs that are proving problematic and need further consolidation.

Name of child	Marvel Towers					CODE Control			
	A Shock for Mini oul short /oo/	A BITE Inside wr /r/ rh /r/	Mission Marvel wh /h/	Race Against Time (w)ar /or/ (w)a /or/ a(lt) /o/ (w)a /o/	CODE's Countdown s /s/ s /z/ ie /ee/	The Last BITE ed /d/ ed /t/	Eye to Eye ng	Stop CODE! y /ee/

Gold band • Marvel Towers and CODE Control • **Phonic record sheet**

Project X CODE Practice and Assessment CD-ROM

Once a child has read all four books in a zone (eight texts in total), they can move on to the **Project X CODE** *Practice and Assessment CD-ROM*, which has been built for independent use. The activities for every zone include phonic and comprehension activities. Across the zones there are also sentence structure, spelling and memory activities.

The CD-ROM is divided into two separate views – pupil and teacher – to ensure the material is easy to access and use. Once you have installed the CD-ROM, you can open the software via the desktop icon.

Pupil screens

1 Pupils simply choose the pupil button to access the practice and assessment activities.

A single click on a zone button will open up the practice and assessment activities for that zone.

2 Pupils enter their name to get started.

3 Each set of activities has a number of practice screens, covering a range of question types and reading skills, so that children can try activities before progressing seamlessly on to the assessment screens.

Every instruction text has audio to help children understand how to complete each activity. From Yellow to Turquoise bands there is also additional audio support within the activities. This level of support gradually reduces as the children's ability increases.

Children can check their answers in the practice screens and try again to ensure they have plenty of opportunities to get to grips with the tasks.

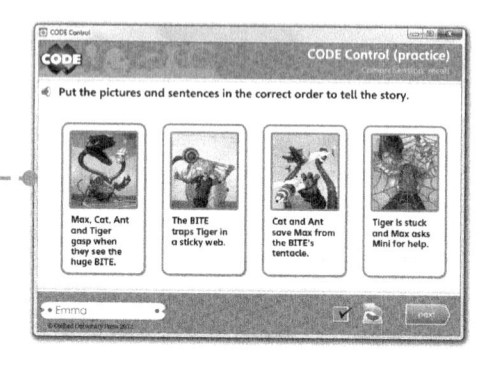

4 Once all the activities have been completed, a report is automatically generated which can either be saved or printed out directly.

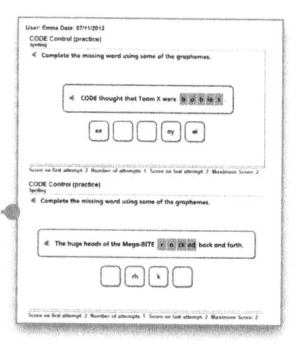

Teacher screens

Project X CODE *Practice and Assessment CD-ROM* provides a wealth of assessment and teaching resources to support your school in delivering well-paced, effective intervention sessions. Simply choose the teacher button to access the materials.

Assessment materials

The practice and assessment activities can be accessed directly from here.

There is a *Practice and Assessment Report Guide* for each set of practice and assessment activities, offering guidance on using the reports.

There are also fully-editable versions of all the assessment materials from this handbook.

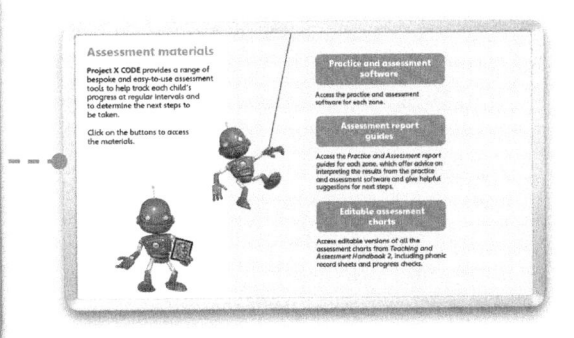

Teaching materials

The Adventure Begins eBook and animation can be accessed here and are the perfect way to launch **Project X CODE**.

There are fully-editable versions of all the PCMs from this handbook, as well as motivating certificates to reward each child's progress.

Additional resources to support every intervention session are provided, including support on running guided reading sessions, clip art, stickers, a board game, collectable character cards and desktop backgrounds.

Getting the most out of Project X CODE

Project X CODE is developed by a team of experts in phonics, intervention, reading engagement and comprehension who have created a series of Professional Development films.

They have also written a guide illustrating how **Project X CODE** addresses the barriers which affect readers, a fully-editable introduction to **Project X CODE** for parents/carers and a management guide for school leadership teams.

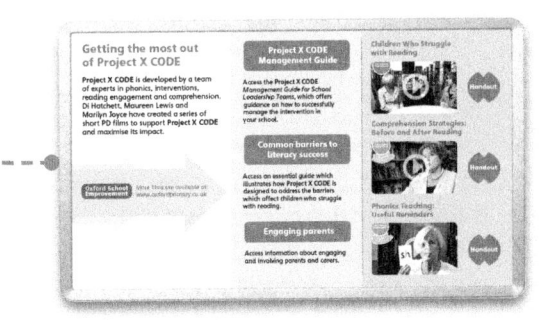

Using the CD-ROM

The **Project X CODE** *User Guide* provides useful tips and information about using the *Practice and Assessment CD-ROM*, as well as practical information about installing and uninstalling the software.

Using the *Practice and Assessment Report*

The *Practice and Assessment Report* is for use by the child's class teacher. It provides a 'snapshot' of the child's strengths and weaknesses in relation to completed independent activities based on content from the **Project X CODE** books.

The report provides an overview of those activities the child has tackled confidently and those where the child has struggled. It shows the screen as the child left it so comparisons can be made between the practice activities and the assessment activities, indicating whether there has been an improvement or whether a particular activity is causing difficulties.

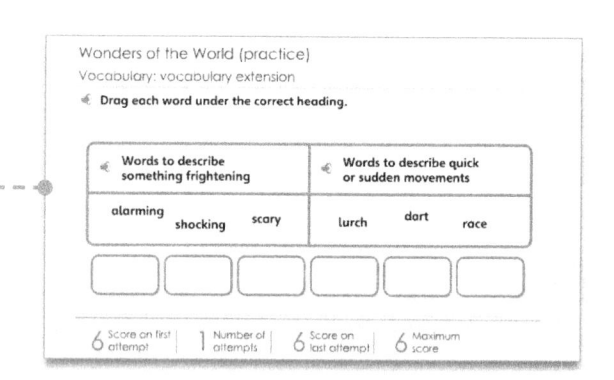

The skills focus of each activity is clearly shown on the report so that further practice can be carried out if necessary, or, if the child has done particularly well, specific praise can be given.

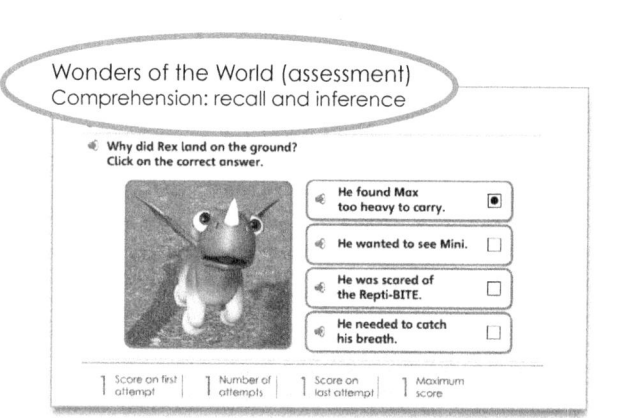

At the end of the report, an overall total is given for the assessment activities. Instructions on how to interpret these results are provided in each *Practice and Assessment Report Guide*, which can be found on the **Project X CODE** *Practice and Assessment CD-ROM*.

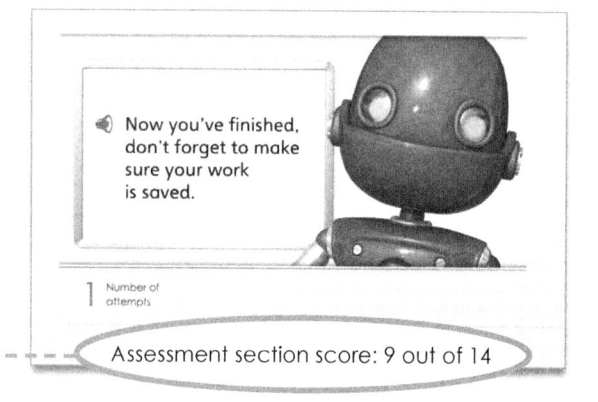

Any evidence gathered from the *Practice and Assessment Report* should be used in conjunction with evidence from both the day-to-day and summative assessments in **Project X CODE**. The report on its own does not provide definitive judgement in terms of the child's knowledge, skills and understanding or progress on the **Project X CODE** programme.

Project X CODE End of band progress check – Turquoise band (Castle Kingdom and Forbidden Valley)

Editable version available on the Project X CODE Practice and Assessment CD-ROM

After a child has read all the Castle Kingdom and Forbidden Valley books, complete the table to check their progress.

Name of child _____ Date _____ Completed by _____

Key knowledge and skills	Comments and follow-up actions
Phonic knowledge • Gives the sound when shown any grapheme from Phases 2, 3, 4 or 5. • Finds any Phase 2, 3, 4 or 5 grapheme on a display when given the sound. • Blends and reads words comprising GPCs from Phases 4 and 5. These should include two- and three-syllable words. • Writes the common graphemes from any given sound from Phases 2, 3, 4 or 5.	
Tricky words • Reads the tricky words: was, were, you, said, some, come.	
Reading check • Automatically applies phonic knowledge and skills as the prime approach to reading unfamiliar words, self-correcting where necessary. • Makes use of decoding when tackling tricky words. • When need arises, rereads a sentence and/or reads on to check that it makes sense, self-correcting where necessary. • Reads with increasing fluency and expression.	
Comprehension When prompted: • Comments on the use of features in a text, such as the use of speech bubbles, punctuation, effective words, e.g. *Look back through the book. Which features belong to story pages and which belong to information pages?* (Forbidden Valley: 39. Volcano Blast) • Shows awareness that stories are set in different times and places, e.g. *Team X and Mini went back in time in the Castle Kingdom zone. How do you think this zone will be different?* (Forbidden Valley: 37. Up in the Air) • Summarises key events from a story in the correct sequence, e.g. *Give a summary of each chapter using just one sentence.* (Castle Kingdom: 33. The Joust) • Makes inferences using empathy, e.g. *Describe how Tiger felt when he first got on the horse and how he felt after the Knight-BITE charged at him.* (Castle Kingdom: 33. The Joust) • Can recall and summarise key facts from an information text, e.g. *What are the dangers you would have to watch out for if you were near a volcano?* (Forbidden Valley: 39. Volcano Blast)	

Turquoise band • Castle Kingdom and Forbidden Valley • **End of band progress check**

Project X CODE End of band progress check – Purple band (Wonders of the World and Pyramid Peril)

Editable version available on the Project X CODE Practice and Assessment CD-ROM

After a child has read all the Wonders of the World and Pyramid Peril books, complete the table to check their progress.

Name of child _____ Date _____ Completed by _____

Key knowledge and skills	Comments and follow-up actions
Phonic knowledge • Gives the sound when shown any grapheme from Phases 2, 3, 4 or 5. • Finds any Phase 2, 3, 4 or 5 grapheme on a display when given the sound. • Blends and reads words comprising GPCs from Phases 4 and 5. These should include multi-syllabic words. • Writes the common graphemes for any given sound from Phases 2, 3, 4 or 5.	
Tricky words • Reads the tricky words: little, said, have, through, eyes, once.	
Reading check • Automatically applies phonic knowledge and skills as the prime approach to reading unfamiliar words, self-correcting where necessary. • Applies phonic knowledge and skills when tackling tricky words and unfamiliar words which are not fully decodable. • When need arises, rereads a sentence and/or reads on to check that it makes sense, self-correcting where necessary. • Reads with accuracy, fluency and expression, paying attention to the cues in the text, e.g. direct speech, use of different fonts and punctuation.	
Comprehension When prompted: • Identifies a few basic features of the writer's use of language for effect, such as their choice of adjectives and verbs, e.g. *What do you think the author means when he describes how the Repti-BITE 'creeps up on its enemies like a phantom'?* (Wonders of the World: 43. Scare in the Air) • Expresses a personal response, drawing a parallel from their own experience, e.g. *Why do you think Tiger ignored the warning sign? What would you have done if you were going on that ride?* (Wonders of the World: 41. Invisible Threat) • Gives and justifies a personal opinion about the text, e.g. *At the end of the story, Ant and Tiger start to think their mission is impossible. Do you agree?* (Pyramid Peril: 46. Another Way In) • Makes straightforward inferences using evidence/quotations from the text, e.g. *Max is abseiling into the stone circle because he thinks it is empty. Is he in danger? Why?* (Wonders of the World: 44. Secret of the Stone) • Summarises key information using their own words, e.g. *Now that you have read about the Mummy-BITE, can you summarise the most important information about how it attacks?* (Pyramid Peril: 47. Rock Shock)	

Purple band • Wonders of the World and Pyramid Peril • **End of band progress check**

Project X CODE End of band progress check – Gold band (Marvel Towers and CODE Control)

Editable version available on the Project X CODE Practice and Assessment CD-ROM

After a child has read all the Marvel Towers and CODE Control books, complete the table to check their progress.

Name of child _____ Date _____ Completed by _____

Key knowledge and skills	Comments and follow-up actions
Phonic knowledge • Gives the sound when shown any grapheme from Phases 2, 3, 4 or 5. • Finds any Phase 2, 3, 4 or 5 grapheme on a display when given the sound. • Blends and reads words comprising GPCs from Phase 5. These should include multi-syllabic words and target suffixes from CODE Control. • Writes the common graphemes for any given sound from Phases 2, 3, 4 or 5.	
Tricky words • Can highlight the tricky part of a selected word and accurately spell the word using Look, Cover, Remember, Write, Check: should, rhythm, warm, wriggled, whole.	
Reading check • Automatically applies phonic knowledge and skills as the prime approach to reading unfamiliar words, self-correcting where necessary. • Applies phonic knowledge and skills when tackling tricky words and unfamiliar words which are not fully decodable. • When need arises, rereads a sentence and/or reads on to check that it makes sense, self-correcting where necessary. • Reads with accuracy, fluency and expression, paying attention to the cues in the text, e.g. direct speech, use of language for effect.	
Comprehension When prompted: • Identifies a few basic features of the author's use of language for effect, such as adjectives to describe an object or experience, and suggest alternatives, e.g. *Choose a word to describe the CODE keys that Tiger is holding. Can you think of any other describing words (adjectives) you could use?* (CODE Control: 55. Eye to Eye) • Reflects on a course of events described in a story and makes predictions regarding likely future events, e.g. *Team X still haven't managed to stop CODE. What do you think will happen next?* (CODE Control: 55. Eye to Eye) • Makes straightforward inferences using evidence/quotations from the text, such as the role played by a particular character, e.g. *Choose to be Mini, Marvel or CODE and read their speech or thoughts. Can you change your voice to sound like that character?* (Marvel Towers: 52. Race Against Time) • Can discuss events in a story, relating these to the point of view of a specific character, e.g. *Imagine you are Max. What would you say? What are you thinking? How are you feeling?* (CODE Control: 54. The Last BITE) • Summarises the main events from a chapter in one sentence, e.g. *What were the most important events in this story? Think of one sentence to summarise each chapter.* (Marvel Towers: 49. A Shock for Mini)	

Gold band • Marvel Towers and CODE Control • **End of band progress check**

© Oxford University Press 2012. Copying permitted within the purchasing school only.

Comprehension checklist

If a progress check meeting raises concerns about a child's comprehension, use this checklist to identify those skills in which the child is secure and those which present difficulties. This will identify specific aspects which need further practice. Discussion about the texts and further oral practice can often be particularly helpful.

Editable version available on the Project X CODE Practice and Assessment CD-ROM

Name:	Comments and date
Comprehension skills	
Can relate prior knowledge to the content of the book	
Makes sensible predictions, supported with evidence	
Confirms/changes predictions in the light of further reading	
Asks own questions of text	
Clarifies unknown vocabulary/phrases/sentences	
Uses visualisation and other sensory techniques to enhance understanding	
Retells sequentially	
Can summarise story/episode/information	
Makes inferences and deductions, including drawing on own world knowledge, when appropriate	
Can synthesise separate information from across a text	
Identifies relevant/irrelevant material (determining importance)	
Can empathise with a character's behaviours/situations	
Discusses author's intentions, e.g. *The author used this word because …*	
Makes personal responses to a text	
Supports views with evidence from the text	
Can take a critical stance, by retelling from an alternative viewpoint	
Reflection on learning	
Can identify strategies they used to clarify meaning, e.g. *I reread it to make it clearer.*	
Can reflect on their effectiveness in supporting their understanding, e.g. *I need to ask if I don't know what a word means instead of ignoring it.*	

End of band reading passages

The **Project X CODE** End of band reading passages support the process of making a detailed assessment of a child's reading strengths and areas for development if the End of band progress check indicates a very close look is needed. They help identify how the child uses decoding and reading for meaning strategies.

You will need:

- two copies of the appropriate reading passage: one for the child and one to be marked up by the adult as the child reads
- a quiet space in which to conduct the assessment.

Before reading

- Explain to the child that you want to find out what they are doing well in their reading and where they might need a bit more help. Stress that this is not a 'test'. Explain that you will be making some notes as they read so that you can remember what they did.
- Mark up your copy of the text as the child reads aloud, using the conventions shown on page 38 to indicate whether the child used decoding and blending, knew the word on sight, reread for meaning, self-corrected or used any other strategies.
- If the child struggles with a word, give them plenty of time to try decoding. Avoid the temptation to instantly prompt them as you want to assess what the child can do unaided. When it is clear that the child is not going to read the word unaided you can then offer prompts to support decoding or supply the word.

After reading

- Give the child some immediate positive feedback, e.g. *You said the wrong word the first time but then you corrected the mistake. Well done!*
- Ask the child the questions to informally assess their overall understanding.
- Analyse the child's reading behaviour and use this evidence to inform decisions about the next steps to take (see page 25).

Analysing the End of band reading passage

It is best to undertake the detailed analysis immediately after a session.

1. Note your general comments about the child's reading of the text.
2. Note the number of errors and self-corrections.
3. Look at the types of cues and strategies the child used when making errors and self-correcting:
   - Are they over-dependent on one particular cue? For example, do they find blending difficult even though they know the phonemes?
   - Was the child confident to attempt words they were finding difficult? How many attempts did they make? Did you have to prompt them?
   - Are there any repeated patterns of errors, e.g. a particular word/phoneme, missing out a word, reading the first part correctly?
4. Did the child understand the passage?
5. Reflect on what this tells you about the child's strengths and areas for development.

How to use the End of band reading passages

Child's reading behaviour	How to record	Example
Child reads accurately	Tick or leave blank each correct word	✓ ✓ ✓ ✓ ✓ Every cloud has a silver lining
Child substitutes another word without any sounding out	Write final substituted word above the word	✓ clown ✓ ✓ ✓ ✓ Every cloud has a silver lining
Child self-corrects after initially substituting a word	Write SC after substitution to indicate self-corrected	✓ clown/SC ✓ ✓ ✓ ✓ Every cloud has a silver lining
Child omits a word	Write a long dash above the word	✓ ✓ ✓ — ✓ ✓ Every cloud has a silver lining
Child inserts a word	Write ^ at point of insertion and the word inserted	✓ little ✓ ✓ ✓ ✓ Every cloud has a silver lining ^
Child correctly repeats a word or phrase (trying it out)	Write R1 (one repetition), R2 (two repetitions), etc. above word. If a phrase is repeated, underline the phrase	✓ R2 ✓ ✓ ✓ ✓ Every cloud has a silver lining
Child rereads a sentence for meaning	Underline the sentence and write m	✓ ✓ ✓ ✓ ✓ <u>Every cloud has a silver lining</u> (m)
Child sounds out all or part of a word	Mark the phonemes correctly read plus √ if word is blended correctly or write incorrect word or G if child doesn't offer a word and it is given	✓ cl/ow/d ✓ ✓ ✓ ✓ Every cloud has a silver lining cl/ow/n clown Every cloud has a silver lining cl/ow/d G Every cloud has a silver lining
Teacher prompting: Child stops after one attempt and does not try again. Teacher prompts them to have another go	Write TP above the word then √ if word read correctly or G if word then given	✓ TP ✓ ✓ ✓ ✓ Every cloud has a silver lining ✓ TP/G ✓ ✓ ✓ ✓ Every cloud has a silver lining
Teacher intervention: Child makes no attempt to read the word	Write G above the word if child is given the word after a 5–10 second wait	✓ G ✓ ✓ ✓ ✓ Every cloud has a silver lining

Project X CODE End of band reading passage – Turquoise band (Castle Kingdom and Forbidden Valley)

Editable version available on the Project X CODE Practice and Assessment CD-ROM

Name of child: _____ **Date:** _____

Symbols:
✓ = correct   SC = self-corrected   − = word omitted   / / = phonemes said
∧ = word inserted   TP = teacher prompt   G = given   _____(m) = reread for meaning

Adult: *Here is a summary of the Castle Kingdom and Forbidden Valley zones.*

Once Upon a Time

You can step back in time in some of the zones in Micro World!

Castle Kingdom

Castle Kingdom has a jousting alley where knights fight. There are cells with strong doors. An army of MITEs is in the valley, waiting for a sign to attack the castle. The CODE key is hidden underneath the sword in the stone.

Forbidden Valley

Forbidden Valley is like the earth a long time ago. It is *not* a calm place! Lava pours out from the centre of volcanoes. If you get caught in the lava, it goes solid, so you ought to be careful. The Dino-BITE's roar is so loud it can give you a sore head, but the worst thing is the temperature.

Oral activity
Ask the child the questions to check their understanding.
In Castle Kingdom, why are the MITEs in the valley?
What would happen if you got caught in the lava?
How are Castle Kingdom and Forbidden Valley the same?

Project X CODE End of band reading passage – Purple band (Wonders of the World and Pyramid Peril)

Editable version available on the Project X CODE Practice and Assessment CD-ROM

Name of child: _____ **Date:** _____

Symbols:
✓ = correct   SC = self-corrected   – = word omitted   / / = phonemes said
∧ = word inserted   TP = teacher prompt   G = given   _____(m) = reread for meaning

Adult: *Here are some questions and answers about Team X and Mini's mission.*

What Next?

What have Team X and Mini done so far?

To complete their special mission to stop CODE from shrinking the world and creating chaos, Team X had to travel through twelve zones. Mini has been their guide. It has been a tough quest and they have often been in peril from ghastly BITEs.

What do they still have to do?

The team are near their final destination, but it is too soon to cheer. They still have to end CODE's reign and rescue Macro Marvel, but they don't know where he is.

How is Mini feeling?

Mini wants to go straight to the final zone so she can find her dad and take care of him. She cannot bear to think what might have happened to him.

Oral activity
Ask the child the questions to check their understanding.
Which word means the end of a journey? Which word means to rule over something? How is Mini feeling?

Purple band ● Wonders of the World and Pyramid Peril ● **End of band reading passage**
© Oxford University Press 2012. Copying permitted within the purchasing school only.

Project X CODE End of band reading passage – Gold band (Marvel Towers and CODE Control)

Editable version available on the Project X CODE Practice and Assessment CD-ROM

Name of child: _____ **Date:** _____

Symbols:
✓ = correct   SC = self-corrected   – = word omitted   / / = phonemes said
∧ = word inserted   TP = teacher prompt   G = given   _____(m) = reread for meaning

Adult: *This is an interview with Macro Marvel about the future of Micro World.*

Micro World to Reopen

Macro Marvel, the inventor of Micro World, announced today that Micro World will reopen. The whole park was closed down on its opening day when CODE went wrong.

Marvel told our reporter: "I want to say thank you to Team X and my daughter, Mini, whose bravery meant we could halt CODE. I am looking forward to starting again. The park is now safe and our marvellous rides are waiting to be enjoyed."

He added, "You are all welcome to come to our reopening party. You can walk around, enjoy fantastic rides, watch a rhythm band, meet celebrity guests and win exciting awards. Come along! You might win a fabulous prize!"

Oral activity
Ask the child the questions to check their understanding.
Which words does Macro Marvel use to make Micro World sound like a good place to visit?
What five things could you do at the reopening party?
Why do you think Marvel needs to have a reopening party?

Implementing Project X CODE

Research has shown that intervention programmes achieve maximum impact when core elements are closely adhered to (fidelity), whilst other aspects are tailored to the individual circumstances of schools (flexibility). **Project X CODE** has been carefully developed with the following core and flexible aspects in mind.

Core aspects requiring fidelity to secure impact	Flexible aspects to be determined by schools
Leadership support	Choice of target group(s)
A teaching assistant trained in synthetic phonics and intervention support	Group size
A link teacher to support the work of the teaching assistant	Choice of entry and exit points for children
Frequent intervention sessions (four times per week)	Timetabling in the school day
Following the 30 minute structure and timings	Scheduling of intervention period
Using the inbuilt assessments and progress checks	Choice of standardised tests to assess impact
Regular dialogue between class teacher and intervention teaching assistant	Links to progress meetings
Involving parents/carers	Effective strategies to involve parents/carers

For further details of the flexible aspects of **Project X CODE**, go to page 12.

Additional resources for running Project X CODE

In addition to the wealth of resources in **Project X CODE**, further materials will be needed to implement effective intervention sessions. In terms of manageability, these have been kept to a minimum and are referenced in the session notes. These are:

- A flipchart or whiteboard and a display board
- A set of phoneme flashcards
- A set of magnetic letters
- Access to a printer/photocopier
- An A4 file or notebook for each child (referred to in the session notes as the CODE tracker file) to store children's work.

Intervention session space

In order to get maximum impact from **Project X CODE**, a dedicated space should be identified which can be used for all the sessions. Experience in schools shows that the more the space can be personalised to the intervention in terms of ready access to resources and the display of posters and children's work, the more effective the sessions will be.

Involving parents and carers in Project X CODE

Parents and/or carers are children's first and continuing teachers. Evidence shows that parents/carers who regularly talk with their children, who read with and to their children, and who act as good 'model readers' themselves, play a vital role in children's development as readers. Of course not all home backgrounds can provide these 'ideal' conditions and some parents/carers may need help and support to become actively involved in helping their child learn to read.

Before starting Project X CODE

Parents/carers should be informed about their child's involvement in any additional intervention. Making it clear from the start that they are welcome to come and see a session in action can often help to dispel anxiety, as can showing them some of the interactive activities involved and, if necessary, reassuring them that they are not expected to read to their children or hear them read every night. Of course, the parents/carers who are confident should be encouraged to read with their children and the benefits of this explained to them. There are editable materials to support parents/carers, including a letter and simple activities to do at home, on the **Project X CODE** *Practice and Assessment CD-ROM*.

During Project X CODE

Project X CODE includes a range of materials designed to help parents/carers get involved:

- **Before and after reading pages** (see page 9): these are closely linked to the content of the **Project X CODE** sessions and are suitable for a child to repeat at home once they have received the relevant session. For children who may not receive such support at home, this could easily be done with a reading helper or a teaching assistant.

- **Takeaway activities**: these include straightforward speaking and listening activities, e.g. 'Ask me about' labels to be worn by the child. These questions are intended to be asked by any adult, including parents, and adults in school should be primed to talk to a child wearing these labels. Some Takeaway activities involve completion of a more complex task which includes reading and writing. At the discretion of schools, these can be sent home or completed at another time.

- **Project X CODE software** (see pages 30–32): the **Project X CODE** *Practice and Assessment CD-ROM* includes practice and assessment activities. There are also fully-editable materials to support parents/carers, including a letter introducing **Project X CODE** and simple activities to do at home, and a parent handout. The **Project X CODE** eBook software includes eBooks and audio narration of all the **Project X CODE** books. Schools will be able to decide how to use this software with parents or other adults.

- **Project X CODE sessions**: schools could ask parents in to see a session or make a video and invite them to view it and discuss what is happening.

- **Oxford Owl**: includes a selection of the **Project X CODE** eBooks, which parents could read with children at www.oxfordowl.co.uk

Project X CODE – Session notes and getting started

Project X CODE sessions are underpinned by certain key features that are known to be critical to success (whether for a whole class, a small group or an individual):

- Teaching is focused and structured so that pupils know what they are going to learn and how it fits with what they know and can do already.
- Teaching concentrates on the misconceptions, gaps or weaknesses that pupils have experienced in their learning to date and builds in additional consolidation.
- Sessions are designed around a structure that emphasises the stages of learning from which pupils will benefit most.
- Pupils are motivated by pace, dialogue and stimulating activities.
- Pupils' progress is assessed regularly.
- Teachers and teaching assistants have high expectations of the effort pupils will need to make and the progress that can and should be achieved.
- Teachers and teaching assistants create a settled and purposeful atmosphere for learning.

Getting started: key actions

Before starting **Project X CODE**, there are a number of steps that should be undertaken:

School leaders

- Read the **Project X CODE** *Management Guide for School Leadership Teams* on the **Project X CODE** *Practice and Assessment CD-ROM*.
- Identify the children.
- Consider the use of a standardised test to track progress pre- and post-intervention.
- Identify the trained teaching assistant to teach the sessions and the link teacher to support and oversee their work.
- Identify the teaching area, timetable the sessions and ensure parents are informed.

Teaching assistant (link teacher/teacher)

- Familiarise yourself with the resources, the background story and the session notes. Prepare the programme resources, including the CODE tracker file (see session notes), for each child.
- Undertake the launch session with the group or whole class.

Guided reading in Project X CODE

There is an inbuilt progression in **Project X CODE** not only in terms of the reading bands themselves, but also the extent and level of challenge in the before and after reading activities covered in the session notes. From Turquoise to Gold bands, the **Project X CODE** books begin to lengthen significantly in order to promote reading stamina and the sessions change to reflect children's growing independence in core phonic knowledge and skills.

The independent reading section in the session notes progresses from children reading pages in turn towards the introduction of guided reading. As a 'bridge' between the reading in turn featured in Yellow to Orange bands and the introduction of guided reading at Gold band, the teacher or teaching assistant running the **Project X CODE** sessions at Turquoise and Purple bands provides modelled reading of part of Text 2 as a precursor to children's independent reading. This enables the children to experience fluent, expressive reading before they tackle the remaining text themselves.

Guided reading teaching sequence

The context and teaching sequence used in the **Project X CODE** intervention sessions is in keeping with that of classroom guided group reading, following the familiar structure of:

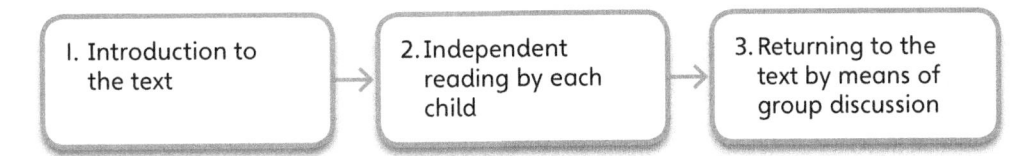

1. Introduction to the text → 2. Independent reading by each child → 3. Returning to the text by means of group discussion

As with classroom guided reading, the children involved are all reading at a similar level and working on a text which presents neither too little, nor too much, challenge for them as independent readers. The role of the teacher or teaching assistant is to 'scaffold' the learning situation so the children can take over independent responsibility for putting into practice what they have learned in **Project X CODE** sessions as well as in their literacy classwork.

Guided reading at Gold band

In the **Project X CODE** intervention sessions at Gold band, children receive additional support in preparing for guided reading through the work they carry out before reading. These are familiar activities, such as:

- **Word alert**: activities to practise focus GPCs and suffixes
- **What does it mean?**: familiarisation with new and challenging vocabulary
- **Into the zone**: for Text 2, this often involves recall of where the story 'left off' in Text 1 and prediction about the plot of the story to follow.

The structured guided reading session takes place with Text 2 in the main, 20 minute part of the **Project X CODE** session, using the familiar structure:

1. Introduction to the text

In **Project X CODE** this involves two elements. First, the teacher/teaching assistant models fluent and expressive reading whilst children follow silently in their own books. Then they briefly discuss some significant features that have arisen so far, demonstrating where the evidence for these can be found in the text.

2. Independent reading

During this part of the guided reading session, each child reads the remainder of Text 2 independently, reading aloud quietly and at their own pace. This does not involve 'turn taking' or listening to each other. The teacher/teaching assistant listens in on each individual reader in turn. As explained in the **Project X CODE** intervention sessions, they will be expecting children to decode successfully without being prompted. If they note any incorrect decoding, they ask the child to check the phonemes in the word again and, if the need arises, to reread the sentence to check it makes sense.

3. Returning to the text

In **Project X CODE** sessions, as children finish reading independently, they are asked to turn to the after reading page and to undertake the familiar activities. This sometimes involves working with a partner. In addition, bookmarks with questions for children to answer when they finish their independent reading are provided on the **Project X CODE** *Practice and Assessment CD-ROM*.

Additional support for guided reading

The **Project X CODE** *Practice and Assessment CD-ROM* offers support in getting the most out of guided reading sessions, including key questions you could ask before, during and after each session. There are also bookmarks which can be given to each child as they finish reading, which will encourage them to explore the book further until everyone has finished.

Menu of activities

Project X CODE sessions follow a set teaching sequence and timings. As the programme progresses through the bands, many core activities are used as a context for learning in terms of both phonics and comprehension.

At Turquoise to Gold bands, the number of phonic Word workout activities reduces to accommodate children's growing skills and allow more time for the longer texts. The main focus is the flashcard activity. The phonic activities children will be familiar with from earlier levels have also been included (see Additional practice and revision activities), to provide ideas for additional practice for children who may be struggling with certain GPCs.

Phonic activites

Word workout activity

Flashcards

Resources: A set of flashcards

Purpose: To improve rapid recall of focus and practice GPCs.

What to do: Show each flashcard in turn and ask children to say the relevant phoneme. Correct any mispronunciation or errors. At the higher levels, use this activity to focus on more challenging aspects, e.g. less common representations of phonemes or phonemes at the end of words.

> **Tip**
> Any GPCs that are less readily recalled can be retained for practice alongside the next session's GPCs. This activity can be given additional challenge by using a timer as children gain in speed and confidence. If some children are struggling to recall particular GPCs, these should be retained and used in every session until they are quite secure.

Additional practice and revision activities

Oral blending

Resources: This is a purely oral activity, without GPC cards or any printed resources.

Purpose: To give children experience of blending phonemes into words so they are familiar with the blending process when they read the words in the story.

What to do: Tell children to listen carefully while you say the separate phonemes that make up a word, e.g. if the word were 'crash', you would say c/r/a/sh/. They have to hear and blend the individual sounds in their heads, then say the word 'crash'. Begin by demonstrating a few practice words, saying the phonemes and blending them into the complete spoken word, so the children understand what to do.

> **Tips**
> Some children are likely to find this activity harder than others, and some may need extensive practice, especially with words comprising more than three phonemes if they have difficulty 'holding' items in their short-term memory. Regular practice will help them to improve, and this in turn will help them to be much more successful in blending the sounds in printed words when they are reading.
>
> **Variation for higher levels:** By this stage, children should be confident in oral blending, so it is no longer a regular part of the sessions. If there are some children who are still struggling with this, select two or three words from the previous text and practise oral blending.

Phoneme count

Resources: Flipchart or large whiteboard and pen

Purpose: Children practise identifying the individual phonemes in words, to develop their phoneme manipulation skills.

What to do: Say or read aloud each word in turn. You could vary the approach by sometimes saying the word and sometimes writing it on a flipchart or whiteboard. Children count the number of phonemes within each word and hold up the relevant number of fingers. Check that everyone is correct. If necessary, demonstrate by repeating the word and raising a finger for each phoneme.

> **Tip**
> Counting phonemes in words spoken aloud (without the printed version) helps to develop accurate spelling. Counting phonemes in printed words helps children to read all through the word from left to right and to 'chunk' words into digraphs and trigraphs rather than letter by letter.

Quickwrite

Resources: Individual wipe-clean mini whiteboards and dry-wipe pens

Purpose: To practise segmentation for spelling.

What to do: Say a word aloud, and ask children to repeat it, saying each phoneme to themselves and writing the word on their whiteboards. Intervene as necessary, encouraging children to check what they have written, making sure they have written a grapheme for each phoneme they can hear.

> **Tips**
> Many children will initially find it helpful to count the phonemes on their fingers (as in Phoneme count, above) as they say the word.
>
> **Variation for higher levels:** This should now include writing multi-syllabic words to make the activity more challenging.

GPC snap

Resources: One set of snap cards per pupil, comprising focus and practice GPCs

Purpose: The game encourages rapid, automatic recall of GPCs.

What to do: Children shuffle their cards and place the set face down. They take turns to turn over the top card and place it on a central pile, saying the phoneme aloud. If their card is the same as the previous person's, the first person to say 'snap' wins the pile of cards.

Sound buttons

Resources: Flipchart or large whiteboard and pen

Purpose: To help children recognise GPCs in the context of whole words and to reinforce their recognition of 'chunks' in words.

What to do: Write a word on the flipchart/whiteboard, saying it aloud. Then mark underneath each GPC, using either a dot for a single letter GPC or a line for a digraph or trigraph. Say each phoneme, with the children joining in, then read the whole word.

> **Tips**
> Split digraphs such as the $\overline{a\text{-}e}$ in 'take' can be marked with an arch to signify they belong together. You could use words from the session's reading text, and include some focus GPCs, which will help children to recognise the GPCs in the context of whole words.
>
> **Variation for higher levels:** Children draw the dots and dashes themselves. This will help them focus on graphemes with two or more letters.

Target phoneme search

Resources: Word list (on flipchart/whiteboard) and pens

Purpose: To help children scan from left to right through words to identify and recognise 'chunks' – digraphs and trigraphs – that represent a sound, rather than trying to blend letter by letter.

What to do: Look at the first word on the list and highlight the focus or practice GPC for that session. Sound-talk the word and then blend the phonemes to read it. Repeat for each word on the list.

> **Tip:** Begin by doing this activity as a group, using a list of words on the flipchart or whiteboard that everyone can see. Ask children to take it in turns to highlight the focus GPC and ask everyone to join in with sound-talking, blending and reading the word. As children get more confident, give each child their own word list to work through.

Countdown

Resources: Word list (on flipchart/whiteboard) and 60 second timer

Purpose: To give children practise blending phonemes in words.

What to do: Display the list of words for the group to see. Ask each child in turn to sound-talk and then blend and read the next word on the list. The aim is for the group to read the whole list before the 60 seconds are up.

> **Tip:** Keep a record of the number of words read each time and challenge children to beat their previous target the next time they do the activity.

> **Top tips for phonic activities:** It is of critical importance that adults teaching children phonics know the correct way to enunciate phonemes clearly and cleanly. It's especially important to avoid adding 'uh' to consonant sounds, making sure they say 'sssssss' not 'suh' and 'nnnnnnn' not 'nuh'.

There are regional variations in the pronunciation of some phonemes. For example: /u/ in southern England is pronounced to rhyme with 'cup', but in northern England, it rhymes with 'foot'. You will need to use common sense and be sensitive to such regional pronunciations.

How to introduce different ways to pronounce a phoneme

There are many occasions where children will need to learn more than one way to pronounce a phoneme or recognise alternative spellings of the same phoneme. Here is one suggestion as to how this can be handled.

What to do:
1. Explain to children that they are going to look at some ways of representing the /ar/ phoneme. *You already know the most common spelling, ar as in hard, and today you're going to look at two other ways of spelling it.*
2. Hold up the cards showing three representations of /ar/: ar, al, a. *In today's story we are going to look out for words with these spellings but before we do, we need to remember that 'a' can be pronounced /ar/ as in hard (southern accents) or /a/ as in hat (northern accents).* Look at the word 'grasped' in Book 35, page 8 and demonstrate the two different pronunciations, explaining that both are correct.

Before reading pages

The before reading activities in each reading book are detailed in the accompanying session notes. In Turquoise to Gold bands, there is a carefully sequenced progression towards more complex concepts and independent learning. Children start by doing activities they are familiar with, such as Sound spotter, but these are gradually phased out and replaced by more challenging activities in the Word alert section. Here are suggestions as to how to carry out the activities.

Sound spotter (Turquoise band)

Resources: A copy of the book for each child

Purpose: To maximise children's chances of successful decoding of continuous text by reminding them to use their phonic knowledge and skills.

What to do: Turn to the specified page, look at the first word and demonstrate how to say each phoneme and then blend the phonemes to read the word. Ask children to join in as you do this again. Read each word in the same way, with children joining in.

Into the zone (Turquoise–Gold bands)

Resources: A copy of the book for each child

Purpose: To encourage recall and/or prediction.

What to do: Ask children the question/s and encourage them to recall what has happened/what they think will happen, as appropriate.

Word alert (Turquoise–Gold bands)

Resources: A copy of the book for each child

Purpose: To prepare for fluent reading by practising the focus GPCs that will be used in the text.

What to do: Refer children to the specified page in the book. Ask them to answer the questions and look out for the words listed as they read through the text.

> **Tip** In CODE Control, the focus shifts to suffixes to demonstrate the relationship between some suffixes and pluralisation, verb tense, adjectives and adverbs. Use flashcards to remind children of the familiar phonemes in the suffixes. Then write the words on a whiteboard and underline the suffix in each word, explaining its effect, e.g. pluralisation, changing a verb to the past/present tense, changing a word to an adjective or an adverb.

What does it mean? (Purple–Gold bands)

Resources: A copy of the book for each child

Purpose: To define the meaning of some words in the text to ensure comprehension is not affected by lack of vocabulary knowledge.

What to do: Look at the selected words given on the before reading page and read the definitions. Occasionally you may wish to ask the children to tell you what they think the word means before reading them the definitions.

Comprehension and vocabulary activities

Many of the comprehension activities used in **Project X CODE**, such as group discussion, sequencing, finding information within the book, and so on, will be familiar to teachers and are therefore not explained here. These instructions focus on comprehension activities that may be unfamiliar to teachers or require more detailed instruction. For each activity children will need a copy of the book.

Shrink the story

Purpose: To develop the skills of determining importance and summary.

What to do: Children are asked to summarise the story in a given way, e.g. one sentence per chapter. To do this they must select what they consider to be the key event/s of the chapter. This can be an oral or written activity as directed in the session notes.

Say, think, feel

Purpose: To develop empathy and inference.

What to do: Children are asked to add what they think might be said by a character, what they might be thinking and what they might be feeling at a given moment in a story. Some of this information is given in the story; they must infer the rest. This can be an oral or written activity as directed in the session notes.

Senses

Purpose: To develop visualisation, empathy and inference.

What to do: Children are asked to consider what a character might hear, see, smell or touch at a given moment in a story. Some of this information is given in the story or illustration; they must infer the rest. This can be an oral or written activity as directed in the session notes.

1 + 1 = 2

Purpose: To develop synthesising leading to deduction.

What to do: Children are asked to locate information from different parts of a text and bring these together (synthesise) to deduce a new piece of information. This can be an oral or written activity as directed in the session notes.

Taking the temperature

Purpose: To develop reflection, empathy and vocabulary knowledge.

What to do: Children are asked to consider the degree of intensity of a given moment/s in the story, e.g. How frightening is this moment compared to another moment? They may also be asked to order a set of words according to their intensity of meaning and reflect on the impact of this.

Why did that happen? (cause and effect)

Purpose: To develop recall, inference and deduction.

What to do: Children link parts of sentences using connectives such as 'so' or 'because'. This helps them recognise and understand the links between actions in a story.

Ask me about
Purpose: To develop speaking and listening skills and recall.

What to do: The child is given a label with the prompt 'Ask me about' to wear after a **Project X CODE** session. This prompts others in the school/home to engage them in conversation on the topic and requires them to recall and articulate what they know on a given topic.

First ... then ... but (cause and effect)
Purpose: To develop recall, inference and deduction.

What to do: Children are asked to recall events and reflect on how subsequent events can cause something to change.

Personal reflection
Purpose: To develop reflection and provide opportunities for children to express personal preferences and viewpoints.

What to do: Children are asked open questions that invite a variety of responses, e.g. *What do you think will happen next? What would you do if you were Tiger?*

Another point of view
Purpose: To take a critical stance by retelling events from another point of view.

What to do: Children are asked to retell the story or an incident from the point of view of one of the characters involved. This can be an oral or written activity as directed in the session notes.

Genre focus/genre exchange
Purpose: To encourage children to use a range of written and spoken genres.

What to do: Children are asked to recall information from the text and present it in a particular way, e.g. an explanation, instructions, description. They may be asked to read it in one genre and present it in another (genre exchange), e.g. read something as a narrative but retell it as instructions.

Why did the author choose that?
Purpose: To encourage children to pay attention to word choice and its impact.

What to do: Children are asked to consider why a particular word/phrase was used and the impact of using alternative words.

Reading in role
Purpose: To develop speaking and listening skills and empathy.

What to do: Children are asked to read a passage in the role of a character or to create an atmosphere. Children will need to reflect on how the characters are feeling and what they're doing, using the text layout and punctuation to guide them.

Project X CODE – Setting the scene

Project X CODE begins with a 'launch session' to familiarise the children with the background story behind the adventures they are going to read. This session is an essential part of the programme and must be carried out at whatever point the intervention sessions start. The gripping launch story, *The Adventure Begins*, will build excitement and interest from the start and can be accessed as a book, eBook and an animation, making for a truly memorable first session using **Project X CODE**.

The Adventure Begins book, eBook and animation can be used with children who will be undertaking the programme or with a whole class, resulting in all children becoming keen to know what will happen, thus boosting the status and self-esteem of those children chosen to use **Project X CODE**.

Project X CODE launch session

Step 1: Tell the children they are going to see and hear about the start of an exciting adventure. (If you already use **Project X**, explain it is a new mission for Team X.) Explain that the adventure is set in an amazing theme park called Micro World, which has 14 zones. Show them the Micro World poster and name some of the zones. Ask them to speculate about what the ride might be for each zone.

Step 2: Before watching the animation, explain that today is the opening day of Micro World and that a large crowd has gathered, including many famous people. Explain the details of Micro World and ask the children whether they think the opening day will go smoothly.

Micro World key information
- To enter Micro World people have to go through the Shrinker to be reduced to micro-size.
- Each zone has worker robots called MITEs.
- Each zone has a BITE which is in charge of the MITEs.
- To leave each zone you must collect the CODE key, which is guarded by the BITEs.
- A computer called CODE controls the MITEs, the BITEs and the Shrinker.
- CODE goes wrong on opening day.

Step 3: Read *The Adventure Begins* to the children or show the eBook on a whiteboard. This tells the story of the opening day in more detail. Discuss the story, making sure children understand what has gone wrong, why CODE has to be stopped, what Team X and Mini have to do and why Mini is going with Team X. Ask children how they would feel if they were Team X or Mini.

Step 4: Show a few of the **Project X CODE** books and explain they are going to read all the exciting stories and find out how Team X and Mini progress through the zones, battle the BITEs and collect the CODE keys.

After Team X and Mini insert the CODE keys in the exit doors, they will need help to read the CODE words. Are the children ready for the challenge?

> **Tip** For those entering the programme later than the initial starting point at Yellow band, use the map to point out the zones that Team X and Mini have already passed through. You may also wish to share the books from earlier levels and to encourage the children to look out for the BITEs and how Team X get from one zone to another. Children may like to read some of the books independently or other **Project X CODE** users could share their favourite stories with them.

The structure of Project X CODE sessions

For every **Project X CODE** book there are two session plans, including PCMs, that offer clear guidance for teachers/teaching assistants. Each well-paced session (30 minutes in total) follows a structured teaching sequence designed to maximise learning opportunities.

1. Introduction:
- Reviews the Takeaway activity from the previous session.
- Helps children focus on the intervention session to follow.

2. Word workout and Before reading:
- Revises and practises the specific aspects of phonic knowledge and skills covered in the book.
- Prepares children to apply these specific skills and knowledge in the context of 'real' reading.
- Provides opportunities for children to explore vocabulary from the text.

At the higher levels, more time is given to reading the text to allow for the increasing challenge of the longer texts. At Gold, the Introduction, Word workout and Before reading sections are combined.

3. Reading the story:
- Provides opportunities to listen to models of fluent reading.
- Helps children independently tackle the graded text, applying the skills and knowledge they have practised.
- Expands children's vocabulary.
- Allows children to practise fluent reading.
- Supports feedback on successful and unsuccessful decoding.

Guided reading sessions are introduced in Text 2 at Gold level.

4. After reading:
- Strengthens speaking and listening skills.
- Supports understanding.
- Takes children back to specific words or phrases and explores these further.
- Helps children remember events and/or the behaviour of characters, ensuring that they refer back to the text for evidence.
- Helps children reflect on events and speculate about what might happen next.

Teaching sequence of each session

Invisible Threat
Purple band
Wonders of the World zone
Book 41

Resources
- CODE tracker files with PCM 81 Wonders of the World zone log
- Zone map
- Wonders of the World zone Book 41 *Invisible Threat*
- Flashcards: eer, ere, ier, ear, air
- Words written on a flipchart or whiteboard: pier, tier
- Phonic record sheet – Purple band (page 28)
- Label only from PCM 82 Cards and labels for each child

Focus GPCs
eer as in steer, ere as in here, ier as in pier

Team X word
Mini

Exploring vocabulary
pier, tier

Wonders of the World
Introduction 3 mins
- If a child is new to CODE, give them their CODE tracker file. Explain that it's a special file to track Team X and Mini's progress through the Micro World zones. Ask them to complete PCM 3 (from *Teaching and Assessment Handbook 1*) as a cover sheet for their file.
- Give out PCM 81 and explain that children will use it to record details they find out about this zone.
- Look at the zone map (on page 4 of *Invisible Threat*) to remind children of the zone Team X and Mini have just left. Discuss the zone they are entering now. Ask children to look carefully at the cover of *Invisible Threat* and talk about what they can see.
- Do you recognise any of the wonders in this zone? (E.g. Eiffel Tower, Statue of Liberty, London Eye, Big Ben, Leaning Tower of Pisa.)
- Draw out the idea that these are some famous landmarks from different parts of the world that people visit. Children may be aware of others.

Word workout and Before reading 6 mins
- Before we find out more about the Wonders of the World zone, we will do our Word workout to get our reading and writing brains working. (See pages 47–49 for details and an explanation of the flashcard activity and other Word workout activities. If any children still need to practise oral blending, select 2–3 words from a previous book.)

   Revise/Practise   Flashcards: eer, ere (/eer/), ier (/eer/), ear, air

- You already know the most common way to spell the /eer/ sound using the letters 'ear' as in 'fear'. In some words, it is spelled differently, for example, 'eer' as in 'steer', 'ere' as in 'here' and 'ier' as in 'pier'.
- Turn to *Invisible Threat*, page 5.
- Remember the sound you have just practised and use it to blend the sounds and read the words.

   Apply   Word alert: steer   here   pier

Reading the story 12 mins
- What do you think the Wonders of the World zone will be like?
- How do you think Team X and Mini will travel around this zone?
- Show the words 'pier' and 'tier'. Read them and explain what they mean.
- A pier is a long, raised platform you walk along, like a pier at the seaside.
- A tier is a level or band in a structure where things are stacked on top of one another, like a wedding cake.
- Turn to page 6 and ask children to take turns reading a page. Remind them to use their phonic knowledge as they decode unfamiliar words.
- Expect children to decode successfully, without being prompted. They should recognise the GPCs eer, ere (/eer/) and ier (/eer/). As they read, use the Phonic record sheet to note words that an individual misreads.

After reading 6 mins
- Turn to page 13.
- Can you explain how the hot-air balloons work?
- Encourage children to look at the picture and explain how you steer the balloons and what the burners fill the balloons with. They can use page 9 to remind them of the details.
- Let's look back at page 11 and read it again. Why do you think Cat sighed when she said she would go with Tiger? (Encourage children to think of other stories in which Tiger takes risks or is too enthusiastic to get going.)
- Do you ever rush ahead because you are excited about something?

Takeaway: talking 3 mins
- In the next story, Cat and Tiger will be exploring the first wonder. It is called the Leaning Tower of Pisa. What can you find out about it?
- Give each child the label from PCM 82. Challenge them to find out more about the Leaning Tower of Pisa and tell someone at school or home about it.

As the book bands progress, the level of challenge increases to move children towards more independence and to reflect the more challenging texts.

5. Takeaway:
- Provides specific opportunities for children to reinforce and practise their intervention session learning in wider contexts, e.g. in class or at home.
- Supports the raising of self-esteem, providing children with opportunities to demonstrate independent knowledge, strengthen speaking and listening skills, and check their understanding.

Key features of session notes

Support is offered in Text 1 to help explain the GPC focus, especially variations in spelling or pronunciation.

All resources essential for the session are clearly listed.

The focus text is clearly signposted.

Invisible Threat
Purple band
Wonders of the World zone
Book 41

Resources
- Wonders of the World zone Book 41 *Invisible Threat*
- Phonic record sheet – Purple band (page 28)
- CODE tracker files with PCM 83 Write a note

Focus GPCs
eer as in steer, ere as in here, ier as in pier

Team X word
watch

Exploring vocabulary (What does it mean?)
chameleon

Additional, not yet decodable words
Pisa, eight, could, towards, floor, stared, warn, chameleon

Tower Trouble

Introduction 4 mins
- Ask children what they found out about the Leaning Tower of Pisa (Takeaway from previous session), e.g. which country it's in, why it leans.
- *At the end of the last story, Tiger was excited about the hot-air balloons. Do you think he will be good at steering the balloon?*

Before reading 4 mins
- *In the last session you practised the sound that you will need to use when you are reading today's story. Let's check that you can remember it as you read some new words.*
- Turn to *Invisible Threat*, page 14.

| Revise/Practise/Apply | Word alert: eerie   interfere   tiers |

What does it mean?
- *Before we read today's story, we will work together to understand the meaning of one of the words we will read today.*
- Read the word 'chameleon' and its definition with the children and check they understand what it means.

Reading the story 12 mins
- *What do you think the BITE will look like in this zone?*
- *Can you remember what happens to Tiger's watch if a BITE is nearby?* (It flashes.)
- Turn to page 15 and read the story and chapter titles.
- *Cat is a bit worried about Tiger steering the hot-air balloon. Listen carefully as I read the first chapter. Think about how Cat is feeling.*
- Read the first chapter aloud as children follow silently in their books. Pause on page 17 to point out the word 'fearfully' and explain that this tells you how Cat is feeling and what sort of expression to use for her speech. Repeat for the word 'sternly' on page 18.
- From Chapter 2, page 22, ask children to take turns reading a page each.
- Expect children to decode successfully, without being prompted. They should recognise the GPCs eer, ere (/eer/) and ier (/eer/). As they read, use the Phonic record sheet to note words that an individual misreads.
- If a child decodes a word incorrectly or is puzzled by a word, encourage them to read the whole word again, looking closely at the sounds in the word. They should then read the whole sentence again to check that it makes sense.

After reading 7 mins
- Turn to page 32.
- *What did the warning message at the beginning of the balloon ride say?* ('Warning! Do not go too high!' – page 15.) *Why do you think Tiger ignored it? What would you have done if you were going on that ride?*
- Encourage children to put themselves in Tiger's place and suggest ideas based on what they know about his character.
- *How did Cat's feelings change throughout the story? Describe how Cat felt in the pictures.*

Takeaway: reading and writing 3 mins
- *Imagine you are Cat and need to write a message to Max, Ant and Mini to warn them about the BITE. What would you write?*
- Give each child PCM 83. Ask them to write a note, using the words on the sheet to help them.

89

Each session is clearly structured with timings provided.

New words are pulled out to help build children's vocabulary.

Answers are provided for closed questions and page references are given if children are required to look back through the text.

The key information for each book can be seen at a glance, including Team X words which children will be familiar with but which aren't decodable in that book, and additional, not yet decodable words included in Text 2 to extend vocabulary.

Questions and information to be told to the children are always italicised.

Editable versions of the PCMs are available on the **Project X CODE** *Practice and Assesssment CD-ROM*.

The Joust
Turquoise band
Castle Kingdom zone
Book 33

Resources
- Castle Kingdom zone Book 33 *The Joust*
- CODE tracker files with **PCM 65 Castle Kingdom zone log**
- Zone map
- Flashcards: ey, kn, y, ng (plus any other GPCs that children still need to practise)
- Words written on a flipchart or whiteboard: jousting, alley
- Phonic record sheet – Turquoise band (page 27)
- Label only from **PCM 66 Cards and labels** for each child

Focus GPCs
ey (at the end of a word): /ee/ as in alley, kn as in knight

Team X word
Mini

Exploring vocabulary
jousting, alley

Knights and Sights

Introduction 3 mins
- If a child is new to CODE, give them their CODE tracker file. Explain that it's a special file to track Team X and Mini's progress through the Micro World zones. Ask them to complete PCM 3 (from *Teaching and Assessment Handbook 1*) as a cover sheet for their file.
- Ask children to look carefully at the Castle Kingdom zone picture on the contents page of *The Joust*.
- *Have you ever visited a castle? Was there anything there that helped you imagine what life was like in the past?* (Displays, historical re-enactments, etc.)
- Give out PCM 65 and explain that children will use it to record details they find out about this zone.
- Look together at the zone map on page 4 of *The Joust* to remind children of the zone Team X and Mini have just left and the zone they are entering now.

Word workout and Before reading 6 mins
- *Before we find out more about the Castle Kingdom zone, we will do our Word workout to get our reading and writing brains working.*
  (See pages 47–49 for details and an explanation of the flashcard activity and other Word workout activities. If any children still need to practise oral blending, select 2–3 words from a previous book.)

Revise/Practise **Flashcards:** ey (/ee/), kn (/n/), y (/ee/), ng (plus any other GPCs that children still need to practise)

- *You already know the most common way to spell the /ee/ sound at the end of a word using the letter 'y'. In some words it is spelled 'ey'.*
- *In some words, the /n/ sound is spelled 'kn'. Look out for this sound when you are reading today's story.*
- Turn to *The Joust*, page 5.

Apply **Sound spotter:** knock alley valley knights

Reading the story 12 mins
- *What do you think the Castle Kingdom zone might be like?*
- Show and read the words 'jousting' and 'alley' together. Explain what they mean:
- *Jousting is an old-fashioned fighting competition where two knights would try to knock each other off their horse with long poles called lances. They would ride towards each other in a narrow passageway called a 'jousting alley'.*
- Turn to page 6 and ask children to take turns reading a page. Remind them to use their phonic knowledge as they decode unfamiliar words.
- Expect children to decode successfully, without being prompted. They should recognise the GPCs ey (/ee/) and kn (/n/). As they read, use the Phonic record sheet to note words that an individual misreads.

After reading 6 mins
- Turn to page 13.
- *Why did Tiger moan when Mini read, "Step back in time"?*
- Encourage children to make suggestions, and explain that Tiger is making a joke, as though stepping back in time is the same as climbing all the steps to the top of the hill.
- *Look back at the story. Which words tell you there might be a battle?* ('Enemy army' – page 8; 'A battle may start at any time!', 'defend' – page 9; 'training for battle' – page 10.)
- *If there is a battle, what might Team X and Mini hear, see, smell and touch?*

Takeaway: talking 3 mins
- *What else can you find out about knights and jousting?*
- Give each child the label from PCM 66. They can tell someone at school or home what they know about knights and try to find out more, for example:
- *Find out which weapons knights used and what they wore to protect themselves when they were jousting.*

The Joust
Turquoise band
Castle Kingdom zone
Book 33

Resources
- Castle Kingdom zone Book 33 *The Joust*
- CODE launch story *The Adventure Begins*
- Word written on a flipchart or whiteboard: activated
- Phonic record sheet – Turquoise band (page 27)
- CODE tracker files with **PCM 67 Finish the sentences**

Focus GPCs
ey (at the end of a word): /ee/ as in alley, kn as in knight

Team X words
Mini, watch

Exploring vocabulary
activated

Additional, not yet decodable words
climbed, castle, want/ed, we're, mission, warning, signal, straight, armour, could, backwards

Knight Fright

Introduction 4 mins
- Ask children what they found out about knights. (Takeaway from previous session.)
- Ask specific questions that will lead into today's story, for example:
- *Which weapons did knights use for jousting?* (Lances.) *How did knights protect themselves?* (Helmets, armour, shields.)

Before reading 4 mins
- *In the last Word workout you practised the sounds you will need to use when you are reading today's story. Let's check that you can remember them.*
- Turn to *The Joust*, page 14.

| Revise/Practise | Sound checker: ey (/ee/)   kn (/n/) |

- *Let's try blending these sounds to read some of the words in today's story.*

| Apply | Word alert: key   monkeying   know   knight |

Reading the story 12 mins
- *Can you remember what Max and Tiger's watches can do?* (Refer to *The Adventure Begins*, page 15, if necessary. Tiger's watch glows to warn of danger; Max's watch acts as a force shield.) *How might they use them in this zone?*
- Show the word 'activated' and check that children understand what it means: made something work by switching it on.
- Turn to page 15 and read the title.
- *What's different about this page compared to other books we have read?*
- Point out the chapter heading 'The Jousting Alley' and explain that this story is divided into three chapters.
- Read the first chapter as children follow, demonstrating how to read fluently.
- From Chapter 2, page 22, ask children to take turns reading a page each.
- Expect children to decode successfully, without being prompted. They should recognise the GPCs ey (/ee/) and kn (/n/). As they read, use the Phonic record sheet to note words that an individual misreads.
- If a child decodes a word incorrectly, encourage them to read the word again, looking closely at the sounds in the word. Then ask them to read the whole sentence again to check that it makes sense.

After reading 7 mins
- Turn to page 32.
- *Look back through the story to remind yourself of the events. Can you give a summary of each chapter using just one sentence?*
- If children are unsure how to do this, demonstrate, for example:
- *I am going to pick out the most important things that happened in Chapter 1. Tiger got on a horse to have a go at jousting but then he saw the BITE.*
- *Describe how Tiger felt when he first got on the horse and how he felt after the Knight-BITE charged at him.*
- Encourage children to look at the pictures to remind them of what happened, and to look back through the book to read what Tiger said. Ask them to compose a sentence orally about Tiger, for example:
- *First, Tiger felt excited, but then he felt terrified because the BITE almost knocked him off.*
- *Can you explain why Tiger's feelings changed?*

Takeaway: reading and writing 3 mins
- Explain that today's Takeaway is a reading and writing activity. Give each child PCM 67. Read it together and explain that they will write a summary of the story by completing the sentences.

Locked Up!
Turquoise band
Castle Kingdom zone
Book 34

Resources
- CODE tracker files
- Flashcards: gn, n, kn (plus any other GPCs that children still need to practise)
- Castle Kingdom zone Book 34 *Locked Up!*
- Words written on a flipchart or whiteboard: cell, gnash
- Phonic record sheet – Turquoise band (page 27)
- PCM 68 Spelling challenge

Focus GPC
gn as in gnash

Team X words
Mini, Macro Marvel

Exploring vocabulary
cell, gnash

The Knight-BITE

Introduction 3 mins
- Ask children to read their completed sentences on PCM 67. (Takeaway from previous session.)
- *What sort of character do you think Tiger is?* (Brave, loves action but sometimes doesn't think things through.)
- *The BITE in this zone is called the Knight-BITE. What have we already seen it do? How do you think Team X and Mini will be able to defeat it and find the CODE key?*
- Encourage children to recall details and make their own predictions.

Word workout and Before reading 6 mins
- *Before we find out more about the Knight-BITE, we are going to have a short Word workout to get our reading and writing brains working.*
  (See pages 47–49 for details and an explanation of the flashcard activity and other Word workout activities. If any children still need to practise oral blending, select 2–3 words from a previous book.)

  Revise/Practise | **Flashcards:** gn (/n/), n, kn (/n/) (plus any other GPCs that children still need to practise)

- *You already know the most common way to spell the /n/ sound – using the letter 'n' – and we looked at one other way when we read the last book: 'kn'. A few words have the /n/ sound spelled in a different way again, using the letters 'gn', and you will be reading some of those words in the story today.*
- Turn to *Locked Up!*, page 4.

  Apply | **Sound spotter:** gnash signs designed never

Reading the story 12 mins
- *How can Cat, Ant and Mini find out about the Knight-BITE? How will this help them?*
- Show the words 'cell' and 'gnash'. Check that children understand what they mean:
- *A cell is a small room where someone is imprisoned; gnash means to grind your teeth together.*
- *This story sounds exciting! Who do you think might be imprisoned?*
- Turn to page 5 and ask children to take turns reading a page. Remind them to use their phonic knowledge as they decode unfamiliar words.
- Expect children to decode successfully, without being prompted. They should recognise the GPC gn (/n/). As they read, use the Phonic record sheet to note words that an individual misreads.

After reading 6 mins
- Turn to page 13.
- *What do you think are the two most important facts about the Knight-BITE? If you could ask the Knight-BITE one question, what would it be?*
- *Turn to page 11. Mini's Gizmo says the Knight-BITE is very cunning. What do you think that means?*
- *Where in the Castle Kingdom zone could the CODE key be hidden? How do you think Team X and Mini will find it?*

Takeaway: spelling 3 mins
- Explain that today's Takeaway is a spelling activity. Give each child PCM 68. They need to identify the tricky parts in the words (from *The Joust* and *Locked Up!*) and learn how to spell them using Look, Cover, Remember, Write, Check.

Locked Up!
Turquoise band
Castle Kingdom zone
Book 34

Rex the Hero

Introduction 4 mins
- Look at children's completed spelling challenges on PCM 68. (Takeaway from previous session.) Talk about the tricky parts in words and children's strategies for remembering them.
- If necessary, practise any words children found difficult using Look, Cover, Remember, Write, Check.
- Remind children of the title of the book.
- *Can you remember reading about the cells? How could you escape if you were locked up in them? What do you predict will happen in this story?*

Before reading 4 mins
- *In the last Word workout you practised the sound that you will need to use when you are reading today's story. Let's check that you can remember it.*
- Turn to *Locked Up!*, page 14.

Revise/Practise	Sound checker: gn (/n/)

- *Let's try practising this sound again to read some of the words in today's story.*

Apply	Word alert: gnarled sign gnat

Reading the story 12 mins
- *This story is called 'Rex the Hero'. What do you think Rex might do to make him a hero?*
- Check that children understand the word 'gnarled': something (usually wood) that is knobbly, rough and twisted.
- Explain that this is another story which is divided into three chapters. Read the first chapter as children follow, demonstrating how to read fluently, e.g. reread page 18, modelling how to add expression to make Mini sound angry.
- From Chapter 2, page 22, ask children to take turns reading a page. Pause at the end of Chapter 2 and ask for suggestions about how Cat, Ant, Mini and Rex might escape from the cell.
- Expect children to decode successfully, without being prompted. They should recognise the GPC gn (/n/). As they read, use the Phonic record sheet to note words that an individual misreads.
- If a child decodes a word incorrectly or is puzzled by a word, encourage them to read it again, looking closely at the sounds in the word. Then ask them to read the whole sentence again to check that it makes sense.

After reading 7 mins
- Turn to page 32.
- *There were different ways that Cat, Ant, Mini and Rex could have escaped from the cell, but there was a problem with each one of them.*
- Ask children to complete the split sentences using the word 'because'.
- Invite children to explain how Rex helped Cat, Ant and Mini escape from the cell.
- *Did anything surprise you in this story? Did you know that Team X could use their watches to make things grow as well as shrink? Can you remember where they have done this before? (In Jungle Trail, Book 20 Wild Rapids, they use their watches to make the Green Dart bigger.)*

Takeaway: reading and writing 3 mins
- *Imagine you are locked in the cell listening to Cat, Ant and Mini discussing different escape plans.*
- Give each child PCM 69. Explain that children will read each character's suggestion and write a short reply to each one.

Resources
- CODE tracker files
- Castle Kingdom zone Book 34 *Locked Up!*
- Phonic record sheet – Turquoise band (page 27)
- PCM 69 Questions and answers

Focus GPC
gn as in gnash

Team X word
Mini

Exploring vocabulary
gnarled

Additional, not yet decodable words
either, doorway, heard, towards, door, we're, floor, great, would, enough, normal

Danger in the Tower

Turquoise band
Castle Kingdom zone
Book 35

Resources
- CODE tracker files
- Flashcards: al, a, sw, ar (plus any other GPCs that children still need to practise)
- Castle Kingdom zone Book 35 *Danger in the Tower*
- Phonic record sheet – Turquoise band (page 27)
- Challenge card only from **PCM 66 Cards and labels** for each child

Focus GPCs
al as in calm, a* as in ask, sw as in sword

(*This phoneme is usually pronounced /ar/ in the south of England. Children with northern accents will not need to learn it as an alternative spelling.)

Team X word
Mini

A Hard Task

Introduction 3 mins
- Ask children to take it in turns to read their answers to the questions on PCM 69. (Takeaway from previous session.)
- *Cat, Ant, Mini and Rex are safely out of the cell, but they still need to look for the CODE key. What do you think might happen next?*
- *Can you remember what the Knight-BITE can do with its arms? Think back to the other stories we have read: we saw one arm turn into a lance but what can its other arms do?*

Word workout and Before reading 6 mins
- *We are going to have a quick Word workout to get our reading and writing brains working.*

(See pages 47–49 for details and an explanation of the flashcard activity and other Word workout activities. If any children still need to practise oral blending, select 2–3 words from a previous book.)

Revise/Practise Flashcards: al (/ar/), a (/ar/), sw (/s/), ar (plus any other GPCs that children still need to practise)

- Ensure children understand that they already know the most common spellings for the phonemes /ar/ and /s/, but some of the words they will be reading today have different spelling patterns, e.g. 'halfway' and 'sword'.
- Turn to *Danger in the Tower*, page 4.

Apply Sound spotter: sword   large   halfway   grasped

Reading the story 12 mins
- *This story is called 'A Hard Task'. What do you think the hard task might be?*
- Begin to read the story together, pausing at the end of page 5.
- *Have you heard the famous legend about the sword in the stone? You might have heard it as a story or seen a film about it. Only the true king can pull the sword out. What do you think will happen in this story?*
- Ask children to take turns reading a page. Remind them to use their phonic knowledge as they decode unfamiliar words.
- Expect children to decode successfully, without being prompted. They should recognise the GPCs al (/ar/), a (/ar/) and sw (/s/). As they read, use the Phonic record sheet to note words that an individual misreads.

After reading 6 mins
- Turn to page 13.
- *Look at all the different words for 'said'. Which ones did the author use in the story?*
- Can you sort the words into two groups: ones that describe characters speaking calmly, and ones that show characters are scared or upset?
- Discuss children's ideas, making suggestions where necessary.
- Look at the pictures of Cat and Ant and read their speech bubbles.
- *Cat and Ant disagreed in the story. Who do you think was right?*
- *How do you think Cat and Ant felt when the Knight-BITE grabbed Mini? Can you explain why?*

Takeaway: talking 3 mins
- Explain that, for the Takeaway, children will practise reading pages 7–9 in the story with a partner, making it sound like a disagreement between Cat and Ant.
- Give each child a challenge card from PCM 66 and a copy of *Danger in the Tower*.
- Challenge children to make up some extra lines for the disagreement between Cat and Ant.

Danger in the Tower

Turquoise band
Castle Kingdom zone
Book 35

Resources
- Castle Kingdom zone Book 35 *Danger in the Tower*
- Words written on a flipchart or whiteboard: anxiously, mace
- Phonic record sheet – Turquoise band (page 27)
- CODE tracker files with **PCM 70 Imagine and write**

Focus GPCs
al as in calm, a* as in ask, sw as in sword

(*This phoneme is usually pronounced /ar/ in the south of England. Children with northern accents will not need to learn it as an alternative spelling.)

Team X words
Mini, Bee-machine

Exploring vocabulary
anxiously, mace

Additional, not yet decodable words
anxiously, could, enormous, couldn't, enough, straight, immediately, action, great

Cat's Master Plan

Introduction 4 mins
- Listen to pairs of children performing their extra lines of disagreement between Cat and Ant. (Takeaway from previous session.)
- *Cat and Ant can't just stand around and argue. They need to make a plan to rescue Mini from the BITE. What do you think the BITE has done with Mini?*
- Check whether children have heard the phrase 'master plan', explaining it if necessary. (It is the main plan, which has a better solution to the problem than all other plans.)

Before reading 4 mins
- *In the last Word workout you practised the sounds that you will need to use when you are reading today's story. Let's check that you can remember them.*
- Turn to *Danger in the Tower*, page 14.

| Revise/Practise | Sound checker: al (/ar/)   a (/ar/)   sw (/s/) |

- *Let's try blending these sounds to read some of the words in today's story.*

| Apply | Word alert: calm   halfway   blasted   answered |

Reading the story 12 mins
- Show the words 'anxiously' and 'mace'. Check that children understand the meanings: anxiously – to do or say something in a worried or nervous way; mace – an old-fashioned club-like weapon with metal spikes sticking out of it.
- *How might Cat, Ant and Rex rescue Mini from the Knight-BITE?*
- Turn to page 15 and read the first chapter as children follow, demonstrating how to read fluently. Pause at the end of Chapter 1 and ask children for their suggestions about what Cat and Ant could do to help Mini.
- Continue reading from Chapter 2, page 20. Ask children to take turns reading a page.
- Expect children to decode successfully, without being prompted. They should recognise the GPCs al (/ar/), a (/ar/) and sw (/s/). As they read, use the Phonic record sheet to note words that an individual misreads.
- If a child decodes a word incorrectly or is puzzled by a word, encourage them to read it again, looking closely at the sounds in the word. Then ask them to read the whole sentence again to check that it makes sense.

After reading 7 mins
- Turn to page 32.
- *Cat's master plan involved using the Bee-machine and the bounce boots. Can you explain how Cat and Ant used them to beat the BITE?*
- Support children in locating the answers, then demonstrate how to put these two pieces of information together by writing it like a sum, for example: Cat used the Bee-machine to blast the BITE with honey (page 28) + Ant bounced up and caught Mini (page 29) = Mini was rescued from the BITE.
- *What has happened to Team X and Mini in the Castle Kingdom zone so far?*
- Draw out the idea that each part of the Castle Kingdom zone is a setting for an adventure, e.g. Tiger and the Knight-BITE in the jousting alley.

Takeaway: writing 3 mins
- Give each child PCM 70.
- *Imagine you are a member of Team X. If you could write a message to Macro Marvel about the dangers in the Castle Kingdom zone, what would you say about what has happened and how you are feeling?*

Battle for the Sword

Turquoise band
Castle Kingdom zone
Book 36

Resources
- CODE tracker files
- Flashcards: st, ve, s, v (plus any other GPCs that children still need to practise)
- Castle Kingdom zone Book 36 *Battle for the Sword*
- Word written on a flipchart or whiteboard: pesky
- Phonic record sheet – Turquoise band (page 27)
- PCM 71 Spelling challenge

Focus GPCs
st as in castle, ve as in have

Team X word
Mini

Exploring vocabulary
pesky

CODE's Plan

Introduction 3 mins
- Read one or two of the messages children wrote to Macro Marvel on PCM 70. (Takeaway from previous session.)
- *Do you think the Knight-BITE is more frightening than some of the other BITEs Team X and Mini have come across?*

Word workout and Before reading 6 mins
- *It's time for our Word workout to get our reading and writing brains working. This will get us ready to read the next book about Team X and Mini.*

  (See pages 47–49 for details and an explanation of the flashcard activity and other Word workout activities. If any children still need to practise oral blending, select 2–3 words from a previous book.)

  Revise/Practise — **Flashcards:** st (/s/), ve (/v/), s, v (plus any other GPCs that children still need to practise)

- *You already know the most common spelling for the /s/ sound, 's', but in some words, like 'castle', it is spelled 'st'.*
- *The /v/ sound is usually spelled 'v', but in some words it's spelled 've'. Look out for some of these words as you are reading today.*
- Turn to *Battle for the Sword*, page 4.

  Apply — **Sound spotter:** leave have castle

Reading the story 12 mins
- *Can you remember why Macro Marvel isn't in control of Micro World? Who or what do you think is controlling the Knight-BITE?* (CODE.) *We will find out a bit more about that in today's story.*
- Show the word 'pesky' and explain that it means to be irritating.
- Turn to page 5 and read the title.
- *What do you think CODE's plan might be?*
- Ask children to take turns reading a page. Remind them to use their phonic knowledge as they decode unfamiliar words.
- Expect children to decode successfully, without being prompted. They should recognise the GPCs st (/s/) and ve (/v/). As they read, use the Phonic record sheet to note words that an individual misreads.

After reading 6 mins
- Turn to page 13.
- *Can you explain what CODE's plan is?* (If necessary, look back at pages 8–9.)
- *How do you think CODE knows what's going on in the zones?*
- Ask children to try describing CODE in their own words. Support them in thinking about what they have read in the story and help them expand on this, using their own ideas.
- *Can you remember any other times CODE has sent a message to a BITE?* (Wild Rides, Book 16 *A Close Escape*; Shark Dive, Book 24 *All Tied Up*.)

Takeaway: spelling 3 mins
- Explain that today's Takeaway is a spelling activity. Give each child PCM 71. They need to identify the tricky parts in the words (from *Danger in the Tower* and *Battle for the Sword*) and learn how to spell them using Look, Cover, Remember, Write, Check.

Battle for the Sword

Turquoise band
Castle Kingdom zone
Book 36

Resources
- CODE tracker files
- Castle Kingdom zone Book 36 *Battle for the Sword*
- Word written on a flipchart or whiteboard: jostled
- Phonic record sheet – Turquoise band (page 27)
- Castle Kingdom zone Books 33–35
- PCM 72 Castle Kingdom CODE words
- Zone map (Book 33 *The Joust*)
- PCM 65 Castle Kingdom zone log

Focus GPCs
st as in castle, ve as in have

Team X word
Mini

Exploring vocabulary
jostled

Additional, not yet decodable words
could, wants, scare, guarding, moving

Into Battle

Introduction 4 mins
- Look at children's completed spelling challenges on PCM 71. (Takeaway from previous session.) Talk about the tricky parts in words and children's strategies for remembering them.
- If necessary, practise any words children found difficult using Look, Cover, Remember, Write, Check.

Word workout and Before reading 4 mins
- *In the last Word workout you practised the sounds that you will need to use when you are reading today's story. Let's check that you can remember them.*
- Turn to *Battle for the Sword*, page 14.

| Revise/Practise | Sound checker: st (/s/)   ve (/v/) |

- *Let's try blending these sounds to read some of the words in today's story.*

| Apply | Word alert: jostled   fastened   glistening   massive |

Reading the story 12 mins
- *The battle is about to start! How do you think Team X and Mini will escape from the battle? What have they got to find first?*
- Show the word 'jostled' and check that children understand its meaning: pushed and bumped roughly against someone, especially in a crowd.
- Turn to page 15 and read the first chapter as children follow, demonstrating how to read fluently.
- From Chapter 2, page 20, ask children to take turns reading a page each. Pause at the end of the chapter to check they have understood the story so far.
- *Did anything puzzle you? What do you think the big shock might be?*
- Expect children to decode successfully, without being prompted. They should recognise the GPCs st (/s/) and ve (/v/). As they read, use the Phonic record sheet to note words that an individual misreads.
- If a child decodes a word incorrectly or is puzzled by a word, encourage them to read it again, looking closely at the sounds in the word. Then ask them to read the whole sentence again to check that it makes sense.

After reading 7 mins
- Turn to page 32.
- *Now it's up to us to help Team X and Mini by reading the special CODE words. These are invented words that we've never heard of before, but we need to read them to open the exit door.*
- Ask children to work in pairs and explain how the Knight-BITE ended up helping Team X and Mini to get the CODE key instead of stopping them.
- Children can then choose their favourite Castle Kingdom book and reread it together.
- While children are working independently, work with each child individually as they read the list of invented CODE words (pseudo words). Check that they can recall the GPCs and blend them to read words. Keep a record using PCM 72.
- *Let's look at the zone map to see where Team X and Mini will be going next.*

Takeaway: reading and writing 3 mins
- Look together at PCM 65.
- *What needs to be completed on this sheet so that you can remember what happened in this zone?*
- Children take the log away to complete at school or at home. They can also take their favourite story away to share with someone.

65 Name _____ Date _____

Fill in the zone log.

Castle Kingdom zone log

These are the dates when I read these books:

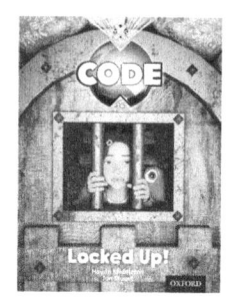

The Joust **Locked Up!** **Danger in the Tower** **Battle for the Sword**

_____ _____ _____ _____

The BITE looked like this:

How scary was the BITE?

5 — terrifying
4
3
2
1
0 — cute

Who was the bravest character in this zone?

☐ ☐ ☐ ☐ ☐ ☐

I think they were the bravest because _____
_____
_____

Turquoise band • Castle Kingdom zone • **Castle Kingdom zone log**

66 Cards and labels

'Ask me about' labels

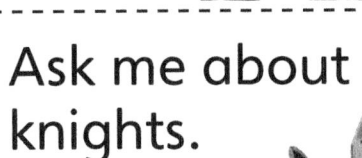

Ask me about knights.

Ask me about knights.

Ask me about knights.

Ask me about knights.

Challenge cards

Read Cat and Ant's speech.

1. Work with a partner.
2. Read pages 7–9 of *Danger in the Tower*. Make Cat and Ant's speech sound like a disagreement.
3. What might Cat and Ant say after Mini was captured? Make up some more lines.

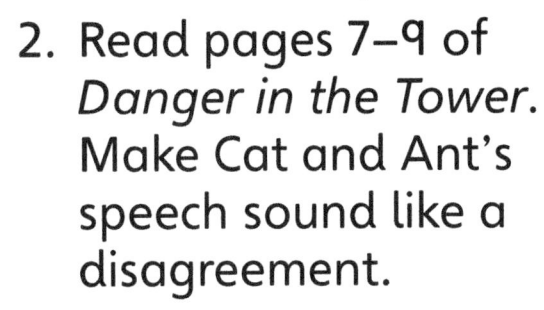

Read Cat and Ant's speech.

1. Work with a partner.
2. Read pages 7–9 of *Danger in the Tower*. Make Cat and Ant's speech sound like a disagreement.
3. What might Cat and Ant say after Mini was captured? Make up some more lines.

Turquoise band • Castle Kingdom zone • **Cards and labels**

Children follow instructions on the cards to complete the activity.

Name _____ **Date** _____

Finish the sentences

Use your own words to complete the sentences.

Tiger wanted to be a _____

He got on a horse but then _____

_____

_____

Max rescued him by _____

_____

_____

_____

Spelling challenge

Follow the steps to spell the words.

1. Look at the word. Find the tricky part.
2. Cover the word. Say each sound. Write the word.
3. Check it is correct. ✓ or ✗
4. Write the word again.

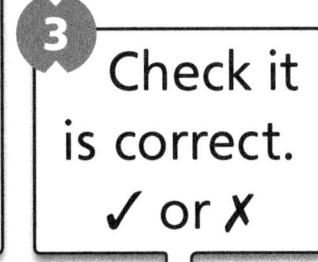

Look	Write	Check	Write
key			
valley			
enemy			
shiny			
knight			
knock			
signs			
gnash			
designed			
never			

Children spell words from *The Joust* and *Locked Up!*

Questions and answers

Read the questions and write answers to them.

Can we bang on the door and shout for help?

No, because _____
_____

Can we shrink and crawl under the door?

No, because _____
_____

Can Rex set fire to the door?

No, because _____
_____

Name _____ **Date** _____

Imagine and write

Write to Macro Marvel to tell him about the dangers in Castle Kingdom.

To: Macro Marvel
From: _____
Subject: Dangers in Castle Kingdom

Dear Macro Marvel,

_____
_____
_____
_____
_____
_____
_____
_____

Children write a message to explain the dangers in Castle Kingdom.

Spelling challenge

Follow the steps to spell the words.

1. Look at the word. Find the tricky part.
2. Cover the word. Say each sound. Write the word.
3. Check it is correct. ✓ or ✗
4. Write the word again.

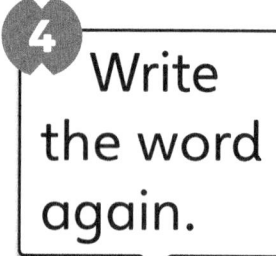

Look	Write	Check	Write
halfway			
calm			
fast			
asked			
past			
sword			
castle			
listen			
have			
leave			

Turquoise band ● Castle Kingdom zone ● Spelling challenge

Children spell words from *Danger in the Tower* and *Battle for the Sword*.

Castle Kingdom CODE words

Help me read the CODE words.

froopey ☐   fama ☐

knool ☐   sworp ☐

gnock ☐   rastle ☐

zalf ☐   paive ☐

Up in the Air
Turquoise band
Forbidden Valley zone
Book 37

Forbidden Valley

Introduction 3 mins
- If a child is new to CODE, give them their CODE tracker file. Explain that it's a special file to track Team X and Mini's progress through the Micro World zones. Ask them to complete PCM 3 (from *Teaching and Assessment Handbook I*) as a cover sheet for their file.
- Give out PCM 73. Explain that children can use it to note details about the Forbidden Valley zone.
- Look together at the zone map on page 4 of *Up in the Air* and talk about all the zones that Team X and Mini have already visited and where they are going next (Forbidden Valley).

Word workout and Before reading 6 mins
🗨 *We are going to do a short Word workout to get our reading and writing brains working.*

(See pages 47–49 for details and an explanation of the flashcard activity and other Word workout activities. If any children still need to practise oral blending, select 2–3 words from a previous book.)

Revise/Practise **Flashcards:** oor, ore, our (/or/), oar, or (plus any other GPCs that children still need to practise)

🗨 *You already know the most common way to spell the /or/ sound using the letters 'or' in words such as 'short'.*
🗨 *Some words have different spellings for the /or/ sound, such as 'floor', 'more', 'pour' and 'roar'. Look out for these words when you are reading today's story.*
- Turn to *Up in the Air*, page 5.

Apply **Sound spotter:** tour   floor   roaring   explore

Reading the story 12 mins
🗨 *Why do you think this zone is called 'Forbidden Valley'?*
- Encourage children to speculate about what Team X and Mini will encounter in this zone and what the dangers might be.
- Show and read the words 'eagerly' and 'erupt'. Explain what they mean.
🗨 *Eagerly means with excitement and enthusiasm.*
🗨 *When a volcano erupts, lava, hot ash, rocks and gas explode out of it.*
- Turn to page 6 and ask children to take turns reading a page each. Remind them to use their phonic knowledge to decode unfamiliar words.
- Expect children to decode successfully, without being prompted. They should recognise the GPCs oor, ore, our (/or/) and oar. As they read, use the Phonic record sheet to note words that an individual misreads.

After reading 6 mins
- Turn to page 13.
🗨 *What dangers will Team X and Mini have to look out for in this zone?*
- Check that children can recall what they have read and encourage them to turn back to pages 8–11 to look for more details.
🗨 *Why did the Gizmo say, 'It's like going back in time'? Team X and Mini also went back in time in the Castle Kingdom zone. How do you think this zone will be different?*
- Encourage children to share what they know about dinosaurs and the prehistoric era. Support them in making comparisons between the time of knights and castles and the time of dinosaurs, emphasising the differences they would expect to see between this zone and the last.

Takeaway: talking 3 mins
- Give each child a challenge card from PCM 74 and a copy of *Up in the Air*.
🗨 *Some of today's text sounds like an advert. Work with a partner to practise reading pages 8–11 like an advert. Record yourself and listen to check that you are happy with it. You could add sound effects too! Then play it to someone else at home or school.*

Resources
- CODE tracker files with **PCM 73 Forbidden Valley zone log**
- Zone map
- Forbidden Valley zone Book 37 *Up in the Air*
- Flashcards: oor, ore, our, oar, or (plus any other GPCs that children still need to practise)
- Words written on a flipchart or whiteboard: eagerly, erupt
- Phonic record sheet – Turquoise band (page 27)
- Challenge card only from **PCM 74 Cards and labels** for each child

Focus GPCs
oor as in floor, ore as in more, our as in pour, oar as in roar

Team X word
Mini

Exploring vocabulary
eagerly, erupt

Up in the Air

Turquoise band
Forbidden Valley zone
Book 37

Resources
- Forbidden Valley zone Book 37 *Up in the Air*
- Phonic record sheet – Turquoise band (page 27)
- CODE tracker files with **PCM 75 Shrink the story**

Focus GPCs
oor as in floor, ore as in more, our as in pour, oar as in roar

Team X word
Bee-machine

Exploring vocabulary
forearm, hoarse

Additional, not yet decodable words
climbing, should, whole, halt, word, travel, normal, heights

Stranded

Introduction 4 mins
- Listen to pairs of children performing or playing their adverts for Forbidden Valley. (Takeaway from previous session.)
- *Do these adverts make you want to go there?*
- Talk briefly about what children have learned so far about this zone.

Before reading 4 mins
- *In the last Word workout you practised the sound you will need to use when you are reading today's story. Let's check that you can remember it.*
- Turn to *Up in the Air*, page 14.

  Revise/Practise Sound checker: oor ore our (/or/) oar

- *Let's try practising the sound again to read some of the words in today's story.*

  Apply Word alert: poorly forearm your hoarse

- Check that children understand the words 'forearm' and 'hoarse':
- *Your forearm is the part of your arm between the elbow and the wrist.*
- *When your voice is hoarse it sounds croaky, rough and deep.*

Reading the story 12 mins
- Look back at the picture of the Big Wheel on page 8.
- *How might the Big Wheel be useful for finding the BITE?* (Team X will see the whole zone from the top, so they might be able to spot the BITE.) *Have you been on anything like this?* (E.g. at a fairground, the London Eye.)
- Turn to page 15 and read the title. Ask children to make predictions about the story.
- *Who do you think might get stranded? How might that happen?*
- Read the first chapter aloud as children follow silently in their books.
- From Chapter 2, page 20, ask children to take turns reading a page each.
- Expect them to decode successfully, without being prompted. They should recognise the GPCs oor, ore, our (/or/) and oar. As they read, use the Phonic record sheet to note words that an individual misreads.
- If a child decodes a word incorrectly, encourage them to read it again, looking closely at the individual sounds. Then ask them to read the whole sentence again to check that it makes sense.

After reading 7 mins
- Turn to page 32.
- *How did Cat and Ant get stranded at the top of the Big Wheel? Can you complete the sentence?*
- Help children to construct a summary sentence using the structure provided, for example:
- ***Cat and Ant wanted** to try to spot the BITE from the top of the Big Wheel **but the BITE** was controlling it **so** it trapped them at the top.*
- *How do you know that Cat was feeling unwell?*
- Help children to identify words in the text that describe how Cat was feeling. ('Dizzy', 'sick' – page 22; 'poorly' – page 26; 'sore tummy' – page 31.)
- *Have you ever felt poorly like that?*
- Encourage children to make links with their own experiences of travel sickness.

Takeaway: reading and writing 3 mins
- Give each child PCM 75 and a copy of *Up in the Air*. Read through the sheet together and explain that children have to think of a single sentence to summarise what happened in each chapter. They may want to use some of the words provided to help them.

Underground Escape

Turquoise band
Forbidden Valley zone
Book 38

Resources
- CODE tracker files
- Flashcards: ough, augh, al, or, aw, au (plus any other GPCs that children still need to practise)
- Forbidden Valley zone Book 38 *Underground Escape*
- Word written on a flipchart or whiteboard: sonic
- Phonic record sheet – Turquoise band (page 27)
- PCM 76 Spelling challenge

Focus GPCs
ough as in thought,
augh as in naughty,
al as in walk

Team X word
Mini

Exploring vocabulary
sonic

The Dino-BITE

Introduction 3 mins
- Ask each child to read one of their summary sentences on PCM 75 (Takeaway from previous session) and check they can recall the main events of the story.

Word workout and Before reading 6 mins
- *Before we read more about the BITE, we are going to do a short Word workout to get our reading and writing brains working.*
  (See pages 47–49 for details and an explanation of the flashcard activity and other Word workout activities. If any children still need to practise oral blending, select 2–3 words from a previous book.)

  Revise/Practise **Flashcards:** ough (/or/), augh (/or/), al (/or/), or, aw, au (plus any other GPCs that children still need to practise)

- *In the last session we focused on different ways to spell /or/. You already know some others as well: 'aw' as in 'claw' and 'au' as in 'cause'.*
- *There are some other spellings of /or/ that are found in a few words: 'ough' as in 'thought', 'augh' as in 'naughty' and 'al' as in 'walk'.*
- Turn to *Underground Escape*, page 4.

  Apply **Sound spotter:** thought   caught   walks   awful

Reading the story 12 mins
- *Today's story is called 'The Dino-BITE'. What do you already know about the BITE?* (That it has sonic blasters behind its head and a control panel on its forearm which controls the Big Wheel.) *What other information do Team X and Mini need to know?* (Where the CODE key is.)
- Show the word 'sonic'. Read it together and check that children understand what it means.
- *Sonic means to use sound waves. The sonic blaster in the story uses sound waves to make a noise so loud it makes the ground shake and hurts your ears.*
- Turn to page 5 and ask children to take turns reading a page each. Remind them to use their phonic knowledge as they decode unfamiliar words.
- Expect children to decode successfully, without being prompted. They should recognise the GPCs ough (/or/), augh (/or/) and al (/or/). As they read, use the Phonic record sheet to note words that an individual misreads.

After reading 6 mins
- Turn to page 13.
- *What three things can the Dino-BITE control in this zone?* (The temperature, the volcano and the Big Wheel.) *Have you seen it using these controls yet?*
- Talk about the BITE's control panel (page 9). Encourage children to think back to the previous story and make predictions about other things the BITE might do.
- *The Dino-BITE is very dangerous, but would it be able to sneak up and take you by surprise? Look back at pages 6–7 and use the clues to help you answer the question.*
- Support children as they use the clues to help them work out the answer: The BITE can't walk quietly (it 'walks with heavy steps' – page 6) and can't conceal itself (it has a zero rating for 'Conceal' – page 7). Therefore, the BITE would not be able to sneak up on you and take you by surprise.
- *Even though this BITE is fierce and strong, at least it won't be able to sneak up on Team X and Mini!*

Takeaway: spelling 3 mins
- Explain that today's Takeaway is a spelling activity. Give each child PCM 76. They need to identify the tricky parts in the words (from *Up in the Air* and *Underground Escape*) and learn how to spell them using Look, Cover, Remember, Write, Check.

Underground Escape

Turquoise band
Forbidden Valley zone
Book 38

Resources
- CODE tracker files
- CODE launch story *The Adventure Begins*
- Forbidden Valley zone Book 38 *Underground Escape*
- Words written on a flipchart or whiteboard: quaking, stalled
- Phonic record sheet – Turquoise band (page 27)
- PCM 77 Jumbled sentences

Focus GPCs
ough as in thought, augh as in naughty, al as in walk

Team X words
Mini, watch

Exploring vocabulary
quaking, stalled

Additional, not yet decodable words
earthquake, heard, scared, earth, searched, here, engine, could, normal

The Quake

Introduction 4 mins
- Look at children's completed spelling challenges on PCM 76. (Takeaway from previous session.) Talk about the tricky parts in words and children's strategies for remembering them.
- If necessary, practise any words children found difficult using Look, Cover, Remember, Write, Check.
- *Team X use a number of different crafts. Today we will be reading about the Driller.*
- Look at *The Adventure Begins*, page 17, and encourage children to predict how and when the Driller might be used.

Before reading 4 mins
- *In the last Word workout you practised the sound you will need to use when you are reading today's story. Let's check that you can remember it.*
- Turn to *Underground Escape*, page 14.

Revise/Practise **Sound checker:** ough (/or/)   augh (/or/)   al (/or/)

- *Let's try practising this sound again to read some of the words in today's story.*

Apply **Word alert:** thoughtful   naughty   almost

Reading the story 12 mins
- *Today's story is called 'The Quake'. Do you know what happens in an earthquake?*
- Show the words 'quaking' and 'stalled'. Read them together and check that children understand what they mean.
- *If something is quaking it's shaking.*
- *We say that an engine has stalled when it cuts out and stops working.*
- Turn to page 15 and read the first chapter aloud as children follow silently in their books.
- Pause at the end of page 18 and ask children where they think Rex is.
- From Chapter 2, page 19, ask children to take turns reading a page each.
- Expect them to decode successfully, without being prompted. They should recognise the GPCs ough (/or/), augh (/or/) and al (/or/). As they read, use the Phonic reading record to note words that an individual misreads.
- If a child decodes a word incorrectly, encourage them to read it again, looking closely at the individual sounds. Then ask them to read the whole sentence again to check that it makes sense.

After reading 7 mins
- Turn to page 32.
- *Look back at page 25. Can you explain how Max, Tiger and Mini were feeling after they fell into the crack in the earth? Why were they worried?*
- Encourage children to express their ideas and help them understand the difficulty of the situation.
- *How did Max, Tiger and Mini escape? Can you think of anything else they could have tried?*
- Talk about the kit and craft that Team X have, referring to *The Adventure Begins*, pages 15–17, if necessary, and explore alternatives, e.g. using the bounce boots, the climbing wires or Hawkwing.

Takeaway: reading and writing 3 mins
- *Imagine that you are with Team X and Mini and using the Driller for the first time. You would need a set of instructions to follow.*
- Give each child PCM 77 and explain that they need to number the instructions in the correct order and complete the sentence about the Driller.

Volcano Blast

Turquoise band
Forbidden Valley zone
Book 39

Resources
- CODE tracker files
- Forbidden Valley zone Book 39 *Volcano Blast*
- Word written on a flipchart or whiteboard: nature
- Phonic record sheet – Turquoise band (page 27)
- Label only from **PCM 74 Cards and labels** for each child

Focus GPCs
Unstressed vowels ('schwa'): re as in centre, our as in colour

Exploring vocabulary
nature

Volcano Facts

Introduction 3 mins
- Look at children's completed sentence sequencing activity on PCM 77 (Takeaway from previous session) and check that they all agree on the correct order for the instructions.
- *Max, Tiger and Mini used the Driller to escape and now they are safe. What else do you think they will have to deal with in this zone?*

Word workout and Before reading 6 mins
- *Before we read, we are going to do a short Word workout to get our reading and writing brains working.*
  (See pages 47–49 for details and an explanation of the flashcard activity and other Word workout activities. If any children still need to practise oral blending, select 2–3 words from a previous book.)
- *We're going to learn about a very special sound today. It's the only one that has its own name: 'schwa'. It's special because it can be made by any of the vowels. I'm going to show you some words from today's story which we pronounce using the 'schwa' sound. Listen carefully and see if you can hear the /uh/ sound.*
- Turn to *Volcano Blast*, page 4.

Apply **Sound spotter:** colour centre cooler

Reading the story 12 mins
- *The title of today's story is 'Volcano Facts'. Do you know any facts about volcanoes?*
- Show the word 'nature'. Read it together and check that children understand what it means.
- *Nature is the name for everything in the world that's not made by people, for example: plants, animals, land and sea.*
- Turn to page 5 and ask children to take turns reading a page. Remind them to use their phonic knowledge as they decode unfamiliar words.
- Expect children to decode successfully, without being prompted. They should recognise the 'schwa' GPCs re and our. As they read, use the Phonic record sheet to note words that an individual misreads.

After reading 6 mins
- Turn to page 13.
- *You read two different types of pages today – information pages and story pages. Look back through the book and find an example of each one. Now look at the table and decide where each label should go – does it describe a story page or an information page?*
- Support children in deciding where each label should be placed.
- *What do you think Ant meant when he said that volcanoes are "really hot and really cool"?*
- Encourage children to make their own suggestions and check that they understand that Ant is playing with words. 'Cool' can describe something impressive, as well as describing the temperature.
- *Do you agree with Ant? Are volcanoes 'cool'? What are the dangers you would have to watch out for if you were near a volcano?*

Takeaway: talking 3 mins
- Give each child a label from PCM 74 and explain that today's Takeaway is a talking activity. Challenge children to find out more about volcanoes and then tell someone at school or home about them.
- *Can you find out about a real volcanic eruption? See if you can discover when, where and what happened.*

Volcano Blast
Turquoise band
Forbidden Valley zone
Book 39

Resources
- Forbidden Valley zone Book 39 *Volcano Blast*
- Phonic record sheet – Turquoise band (page 27)
- CODE tracker files with **PCM 78 Missing words**

Focus GPCs
Unstressed vowels ('schwa'): re as in centre, our as in colour

Exploring vocabulary
vapour

Additional, not yet decodable words
eerie, could, dinosaur, heard, metres, stared, straight, towards

Set in Stone

Introduction 4 mins
- Ask children what they found out about volcanoes. (Takeaway from previous session.)
- *Can you tell me about any famous volcanic eruptions?*

Before reading 4 mins
- *In the last Word workout you practised the sound you will need to use when you are reading today's story. Let's check that you can remember it.*
- Turn to *Volcano Blast*, page 14.

| Revise/Practise | Sound checker: re (/uh/)   our (/uh/) |

- *Let's practise the 'schwa' sound again to read some of the words in today's story.*

| Apply | Word alert: fire   entire   vapour   humour |

Reading the story 12 mins
- *Can you remember who has just walked along the path to the volcano? (Cat and Ant.) Do you think the others know that Cat and Ant came this way?*
- Check that children understand the word 'vapour': steam, mist or smoke that makes a cloud in the air.
- Turn to page 15 and read the first chapter aloud as children follow silently in their books. Pause after page 19.
- *At first Tiger was worried about the mysterious shape, then he was relieved that it was just a signpost. But how is he feeling now? What do you think is making the noise?*
- From Chapter 2, page 20, ask children to take turns reading a page each.
- Expect them to decode successfully, without being prompted. They should recognise the 'schwa' GPCs re and our. As they read, use the Phonic record sheet to note words that an individual misreads.
- If a child decodes a word incorrectly, encourage them to read it again, looking closely at the individual sounds. Then ask them to read the whole sentence again to check that it makes sense.

After reading 7 mins
- Turn to page 32.
- *Why did Cat and Ant yell in terror when the lava sloshed around them? How would you have felt if you were there?*
- Encourage children to suggest their own ideas and draw out the fact that the lava isn't boiling hot because the volcano isn't real – it's part of Micro World.
- *Can you complete each sentence with the word 'liquid' or 'solid' to explain what happened in the story?*
- Help children to read each sentence and choose the correct word. Check they understand that a substance can melt and become liquid when it gets hot and then set solid and hard when it cools down, e.g. chocolate.

Takeaway: reading and writing 3 mins
- Give each child PCM 78.
- To retell the story, children need to choose the correct word to complete each sentence. They then complete the final sentence in their own words.

Dino Danger
Turquoise band
Forbidden Valley zone
Book 40

Resources
- CODE tracker files
- Flashcards: ear, (w)or, ir (plus any other GPCs that children still need to practise)
- Forbidden Valley zone Book 40 *Dino Danger*
- Word written on a flipchart or whiteboard: scorching
- Phonic record sheet – Turquoise band (page 27)
- PCM 79 Spelling challenge

Focus GPCs
ear as in earth, (w)or as in worst

Team X word
Mini

Exploring vocabulary
scorching

Open Wide!

Introduction 3 mins
- Listen to children's completed sentences on PCM 78 (Takeaway from previous session) and talk about the different ways the Dino-BITE has already tried to stop Team X and Mini.
- 💬 What do you think the weather is like in the Forbidden Valley zone? How do you feel if you get too hot? What do you think will happen to Team X and Mini if they get too hot?

Word workout and Before reading 6 mins
- 💬 We are going to do a short Word workout to get our reading and writing brains working before we start reading the next story.
- (See pages 47–49 for details and an explanation of the flashcard activity and other Word workout activities. If any children still need to practise oral blending, select 2–3 words from a previous book.)

Revise/Practise Flashcards: ear (/ur/), (w)or (/ur/), ir (plus any other GPCs that children still need to practise)

- 💬 You already know the most common way to spell /ur/ using the letters 'ir' in words like 'first'.
- 💬 Some words have different ways to spell /ur/, such as 'earth' and 'worst'. Look out for words with this sound as you are reading today's story.
- Turn to *Dino Danger*, page 4.

Apply Sound spotter: earth   worth   words   searching

Reading the story 12 mins
- 💬 What do you think the Dino-BITE will do next?
- Show the word 'scorching'. Read it together and check that children know what it means.
- 💬 When something is scorching, it is very hot.
- Turn to page 5 and ask children to take turns reading a page. Remind them to use their phonic knowledge as they decode unfamiliar words.
- Expect children to decode successfully, without being prompted. They should recognise the GPCs ear (/ur/) and (w)or (/ur/). As they read, use the Phonic record sheet to note words that an individual misreads.

After reading 6 mins
- Turn to page 13.
- 💬 Look back at page 12. Can you find the word that describes how Ant was speaking? ('Panting'.) Try reading Ant's words again to make it sound as though he's been running.
- 💬 On page 9 it says that Rex 'flew for all he was worth'. What do you think this means?
- Help children understand that this expression means that someone is using as much effort as they can.
- 💬 Rex was flying as fast as he possibly could to escape the Dino-BITE.
- Help children consolidate their understanding by using the expression in another sentence, for example:
- 💬 The Dino-BITE roared for all he was worth.

Takeaway: spelling 3 mins
- Explain that today's Takeaway is a spelling activity. Give each child PCM 79. They need to identify the tricky parts in the words (from *Volcano Blast* and *Dino Danger*) and learn how to spell them using Look, Cover, Remember, Write, Check.

Dino Danger

Turquoise band
Forbidden Valley zone
Book 40

Resources
- CODE tracker files
- Forbidden Valley zone Book 40 *Dino Danger*
- Phonic record sheet – Turquoise band (page 27)
- Forbidden Valley zone Books 37–39
- PCM 80 Forbidden Valley CODE words
- Zone map (Book 37 *Up in the Air*)
- PCM 73 Forbidden Valley zone log

Focus GPCs
ear as in earth, (w)or as in worst

Team X word
Mini

Exploring vocabulary
unearthly

Additional, not yet decodable words
tough, signal, guide, towards, straight, dare, want

Tripped Up

Introduction 4 mins
- Look at children's completed spelling challenges on PCM 79. (Takeaway from previous session.) Talk about the tricky parts in words and children's strategies for remembering them.
- If necessary, practise any words children found difficult using Look, Cover, Remember, Write, Check.
- *Do you think Team X and Mini will get the CODE key this time? How might they do it?*
- Ask children to make predictions and then have a look at the title of the story, 'Tripped Up'.
- *Who do you think will trip up?*

Before reading 4 mins
- *In the last Word workout you practised the sound you will need to use when you are reading today's story. Let's check that you can remember it.*
- Turn to *Dino Danger*, page 14.

| Revise/Practise | Sound checker: ear (/ur/) (w)or (/ur/) |

- *Let's try practising this sound again to read some of the words in today's story.*

| Apply | Word alert: unearthly search worthless worm |

Reading the story 12 mins
- *Can you remember why the zone is getting hotter and hotter? (Because the Dino-BITE is turning up the temperature.)*
- Check that children understand the word 'unearthly': something mysterious that seems as though it's not from this world.
- Turn to page 15 and read the first chapter aloud as children follow silently.
- Pause at the end of page 19 and ask children for their opinions about Max's plan.
- *Would you be brave enough to make the Dino-BITE chase you?*
- From Chapter 2, page 20, ask children to take turns reading a page each.
- Expect them to decode successfully, without being prompted. They should recognise the GPCs ear (/ur/) and (w)or (/ur/). As they read, use the Phonic record sheet to note words that an individual misreads.
- If a child decodes a word incorrectly, encourage them to read it again, looking closely at the individual sounds. Then ask them to read the whole sentence again to check that it makes sense.

After reading 7 mins
- Turn to page 32.
- *Now it's up to us to help Team X and Mini by reading the special CODE words. These are invented words that we've never heard of before, but the CODE computer needs them to open the exit door.*
- Ask children to work in pairs and explain how Max's plan worked.
- They can then choose their favourite Forbidden Valley book and reread it together.
- While children are working independently, work with each child individually as they read the list of invented CODE words (pseudo words). Check that they can recall the GPCs and blend them to read words. Keep a record using PCM 80.
- *Let's look at the zone map to see where Team X and Mini will be going next.*

Takeaway: reading and writing 3 mins
- Look together at PCM 73.
- *What needs to be completed on this sheet so that you can remember what happened in this zone? Who do you think was the bravest this time?*
- Children take the log away to complete at school or at home. They can also take their favourite story away to share with someone.

73 Name _____ Date _____

Fill in the zone log.

Forbidden Valley zone log

These are the dates when I read these books:

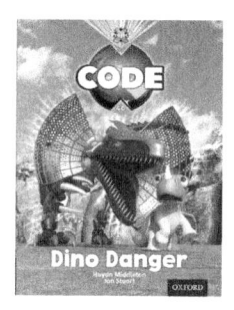

Up in the Air   **Underground Escape**   **Volcano Blast**   **Dino Danger**

_____ _____ _____ _____

The BITE looked like this:

How scary was the BITE?

5 ← terrifying
4
3
2
1
0 ← cute

Who was the bravest character in this zone?

☐ ☐ ☐ ☐ ☐ ☐

I think they were the bravest because _____

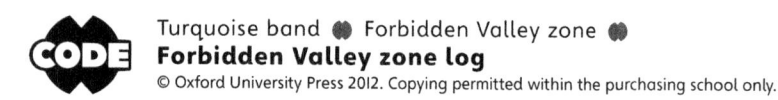

_____

_____

Turquoise band ● Forbidden Valley zone ●
Forbidden Valley zone log
© Oxford University Press 2012. Copying permitted within the purchasing school only.

Children complete a reading record as they progress through the Forbidden Valley zone.

74 Cards and labels

Challenge cards

Record an advert for Forbidden Valley.

1. Read pages 8–11 of *Up in the Air*. Try to make it sound like an advert.
2. Record your reading.
3. Play it back. Check you are happy with it.
4. Ask someone to listen to it.

Record an advert for Forbidden Valley.

1. Read pages 8–11 of *Up in the Air*. Try to make it sound like an advert.
2. Record your reading.
3. Play it back. Check you are happy with it.
4. Ask someone to listen to it.

'Ask me about' labels

Ask me about volcanoes.

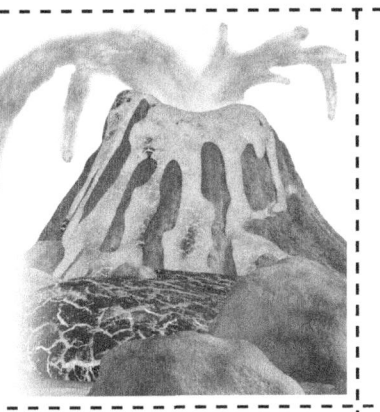

Ask me about volcanoes.

Ask me about volcanoes.

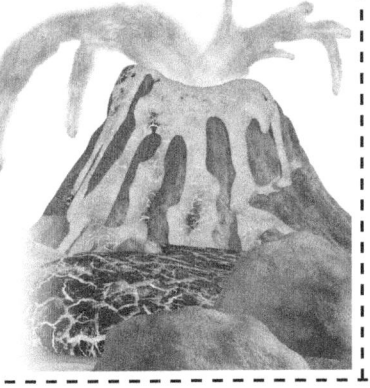

Ask me about volcanoes.

Children follow instructions on the cards to complete the activity.

Shrink the story

Look back at 'Stranded'. Write one sentence to summarise each chapter.
Use some of the words to help you.

Words to help you

Chapter 1 – A Strange Noise
_____
_____
_____

Big Wheel
BITE
noise

Chapter 2 – Sitting Targets!
_____
_____
_____

roar
whizzed
trapped

Chapter 3 – We Want to Get Off!
_____
_____
_____

poorly
Bee-machine
shrank

Spelling challenge

Follow the steps to spell the words.

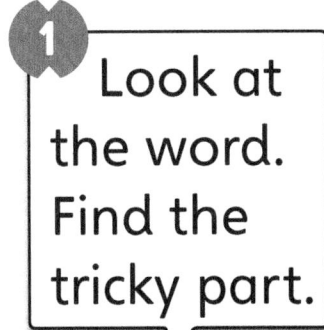

1. Look at the word. Find the tricky part.
2. Cover the word. Say each sound. Write the word.
3. Check it is correct. ✓ or ✗
4. Write the word again.

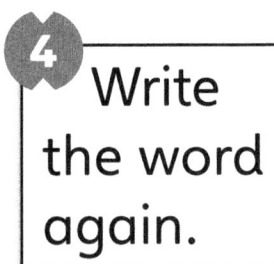

Look	Write	Check	Write
trapdoor			
more			
your			
roar			
board			
thought			
caught			
walks			
talking			
awful			

Turquoise band ● Forbidden Valley zone ● Spelling challenge

Children spell words from *Up in the Air* and *Underground Escape*.

77 Name _____ Date _____

Jumbled sentences

Read the instructions for how to use the Driller and number them in the right order.

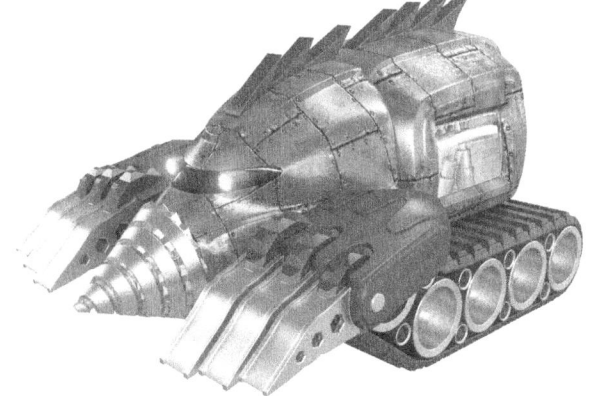

☐ Press the button to start the engine.

☐ Finally, grow back to normal size.

☐ Use the Driller to drill through the earth.

☐ First, shrink to fit inside the Driller.

Finish the sentence.

The Driller is useful when _____

_____

_____

Missing words

Fill in the gaps using the words.

run   erupt   hard   volcano   lava

Cat and Ant were exploring the _____.

The Dino-BITE made the volcano _____ and _____ poured out.

Cat and Ant tried to _____ away but they got covered in lava.

The lava turned _____ so they could not escape.

What did Rex do? Finish the sentence.

Rex saved Cat and Ant by _____

79 Name _____ Date _____

Spelling challenge

Follow the steps to spell the words.

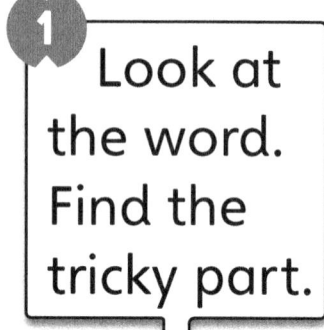

1 Look at the word. Find the tricky part.

2 Cover the word. Say each sound. Write the word.

3 Check it is correct. ✓ or ✗

4 Write the word again.

Look	Write	Check	Write
centre			
metres			
behaviour			
colour			
cooler			
searching			
learned			
earth			
words			
worth			

Turquoise band • Forbidden Valley zone • **Spelling challenge**

Children spell words from *Volcano Blast* and *Dino Danger*.

Forbidden Valley CODE words

Help me read the CODE words.

bloor	☐	skalk	☐
lought	☐	lantre	☐
flaught	☐	lamour	☐
trore	☐	earsh	☐
voar	☐	worly	☐

Invisible Threat

Purple band
Wonders of the World zone
Book 41

Resources
- CODE tracker files with **PCM 81 Wonders of the World zone log**
- Zone map
- Wonders of the World zone Book 41 *Invisible Threat*
- Flashcards: eer, ere, ier, ear, air
- Words written on a flipchart or whiteboard: pier, tier
- Phonic record sheet – Purple band (page 28)
- Label only from **PCM 82 Cards and labels** for each child

Focus GPCs
eer as in steer, ere as in here, ier as in pier

Team X word
Mini

Exploring vocabulary
pier, tier

Wonders of the World

Introduction 3 mins
- If a child is new to CODE, give them their CODE tracker file. Explain that it's a special file to track Team X and Mini's progress through the Micro World zones. Ask them to complete PCM 3 (from *Teaching and Assessment Handbook 1*) as a cover sheet for their file.
- Give out PCM 81 and explain that children will use it to record details they find out about this zone.
- Look at the zone map (on page 4 of *Invisible Threat*) to remind children of the zone Team X and Mini have just left. Discuss the zone they are entering now. Ask children to look carefully at the cover of *Invisible Threat* and talk about what they can see.
- *Do you recognise any of the wonders in this zone?* (E.g. Eiffel Tower, Statue of Liberty, London Eye, Big Ben, Leaning Tower of Pisa.)
- Draw out the idea that these are some famous landmarks from different parts of the world that people visit. Children may be aware of others.

Word workout and Before reading 6 mins
- *Before we find out more about the Wonders of the World zone, we will do our Word workout to get our reading and writing brains working.*
  (See pages 47–49 for details and an explanation of the flashcard activity and other Word workout activities. If any children still need to practise oral blending, select 2–3 words from a previous book.)

  Revise/Practise   Flashcards: eer, ere (/eer/), ier (/eer/), ear, air

- *You already know the most common way to spell the /eer/ sound using the letters 'ear' as in 'fear'. In some words, it is spelled differently, for example, 'eer' as in 'steer', 'ere' as in 'here' and 'ier' as in 'pier'.*
- Turn to *Invisible Threat*, page 5.
- *Remember the sound you have just practised and use it to blend the sounds and read the words.*

  Apply   Word alert: steer   here   pier

Reading the story 12 mins
- *What do you think the Wonders of the World zone will be like?*
- *How do you think Team X and Mini will travel around this zone?*
- Show the words 'pier' and 'tier'. Read them and explain what they mean.
- *A pier is a long, raised platform you walk along, like a pier at the seaside.*
- *A tier is a level or band in a structure where things are stacked on top of one another, like a wedding cake.*
- Turn to page 6 and ask children to take turns reading a page. Remind them to use their phonic knowledge as they decode unfamiliar words.
- Expect children to decode successfully, without being prompted. They should recognise the GPCs eer, ere (/eer/) and ier (/eer/). As they read, use the Phonic record sheet to note words that an individual misreads.

After reading 6 mins
- Turn to page 13.
- *Can you explain how the hot-air balloons work?*
- Encourage children to look at the picture and explain how you steer the balloons and what the burners fill the balloons with. They can use page 9 to remind them of the details.
- *Let's look back at page 11 and read it again. Why do you think Cat sighed when she said she would go with Tiger?* (Encourage children to think of other stories in which Tiger takes risks or is too enthusiastic to get going.)
- *Do you ever rush ahead because you are excited about something?*

Takeaway: talking 3 mins
- *In the next story, Cat and Tiger will be exploring the first wonder. It is called the Leaning Tower of Pisa. What can you find out about it?*
- Give each child the label from PCM 82. Challenge them to find out more about the Leaning Tower of Pisa and tell someone at school or home about it.

Invisible Threat

Purple band
Wonders of the World zone
Book 41

Resources
- Wonders of the World zone Book 41 *Invisible Threat*
- Phonic record sheet – Purple band (page 28)
- CODE tracker files with **PCM 83 Write a note**

Focus GPCs
eer as in steer, ere as in here, ier as in pier

Team X word
watch

Exploring vocabulary (What does it mean?)
chameleon

Additional, not yet decodable words
Pisa, eight, could, towards, floor, stared, warn, chameleon

Tower Trouble

Introduction 4 mins
- Ask children what they found out about the Leaning Tower of Pisa (Takeaway from previous session), e.g. which country it's in, why it leans.
- *At the end of the last story, Tiger was excited about the hot-air balloons. Do you think he will be good at steering the balloon?*

Before reading 4 mins
- *In the last session you practised the sound that you will need to use when you are reading today's story. Let's check that you can remember it as you read some new words.*
- Turn to *Invisible Threat*, page 14.

| Revise/Practise/Apply | Word alert: eerie   interfere   tiers |

What does it mean?
- *Before we read today's story, we will work together to understand the meaning of one of the words we will read today.*
- Read the word 'chameleon' and its definition with the children and check they understand what it means.

Reading the story 12 mins
- *What do you think the BITE will look like in this zone?*
- *Can you remember what happens to Tiger's watch if a BITE is nearby?* (It flashes.)
- Turn to page 15 and read the story and chapter titles.
- *Cat is a bit worried about Tiger steering the hot-air balloon. Listen carefully as I read the first chapter. Think about how Cat is feeling.*
- Read the first chapter aloud as children follow silently in their books. Pause on page 17 to point out the word 'fearfully' and explain that this tells you how Cat is feeling and what sort of expression to use for her speech. Repeat for the word 'sternly' on page 18.
- From Chapter 2, page 22, ask children to take turns reading a page each.
- Expect children to decode successfully, without being prompted. They should recognise the GPCs eer, ere (/eer/) and ier (/eer/). As they read, use the Phonic record sheet to note words that an individual misreads.
- If a child decodes a word incorrectly or is puzzled by a word, encourage them to read the whole word again, looking closely at the sounds in the word. They should then read the whole sentence again to check that it makes sense.

After reading 7 mins
- Turn to page 32.
- *What did the warning message at the beginning of the balloon ride say?* ('Warning! Do not go too high!' – page 15.) *Why do you think Tiger ignored it? What would you have done if you were going on that ride?*
- Encourage children to put themselves in Tiger's place and suggest ideas based on what they know about his character.
- *How did Cat's feelings change throughout the story? Describe how Cat felt in the pictures.*

Takeaway: reading and writing 3 mins
- *Imagine you are Cat and need to write a message to Max, Ant and Mini to warn them about the BITE. What would you write?*
- Give each child PCM 83. Ask them to write a note, using the words on the sheet to help them.

Statue Surprise

Purple band
Wonders of the World zone
Book 42

Resources
- CODE tracker files
- Flashcards: gh, gu, mb, s, g, m, mm
- Wonders of the World zone Book 42 *Statue Surprise*
- Words written on a flipchart or whiteboard: gherkin, ghastly
- Phonic record sheet – Purple band (page 28)
- Wonders of the World zone Book 41 *Invisible Threat*
- PCM 84 Spelling challenge

Focus GPCs
gh as in ghostly, gu as in guess, mb as in thumb, (silent) s as in island

Team X word
Mini

Exploring vocabulary
gherkin, ghastly

The Search Begins

Introduction 3 mins
- Invite one or two children to read their completed notes on PCM 83 aloud. (Takeaway from previous session.)
- *Why do you think it was so important to warn the others about the BITE?*

Word workout and Before reading 6 mins
- *We are going to do a short Word workout to get our reading and writing brains working.*
  (See pages 47–49 for details and an explanation of the flashcard activity and other Word workout activities. If any children still need to practise oral blending, select 2–3 words from a previous book.)

Revise/Practise — **Flashcards:** gh (/g/), gu (/g/), mb (/m/), (silent) s, g, m, mm

- *You already know that 'g' is the most common way to spell the /g/ sound. There are some other ways to spell it, such as 'gh' as in 'ghostly' and 'gu' as in 'guess'.*
- *You also know that 'm' is the most common way to spell the /m/ sound. However, in a few words it is spelled 'mb' as in 'thumb'.*
- *A few words have a silent 's', such as 'island'. We don't pronounce the 's'.*
- Turn to *Statue Surprise*, page 4.
- *Remember the sounds you have just practised and use them to blend the sounds and read the words.*

Apply — **Word alert:** ghastly guess climb island

Reading the story 12 mins
- *Max, Ant and Mini are about to see the Statue of Liberty. What do you know about it?* (E.g. it is in the United States of America.)
- *How do you think Max, Ant and Mini would describe the Statue of Liberty?*
- *Where do you think the BITE is now?*
- *Before we start reading, we need to look at some words that you may not be familiar with.*
- Show the words 'gherkin' and 'ghastly'. Read them together and check that children understand what they mean.
- *Gherkins are small pickled cucumbers. Some people have them in burgers.*
- *If something is ghastly it is horrible.*
- *How do you think these words might come into today's story?*
- Turn to page 5 and ask children to take turns reading a page each. Remind them to use their phonic knowledge as they decode unfamiliar words.
- Expect children to decode successfully, without being prompted. They should recognise the GPCs gh (/g/), gu (/g/), mb (/m/) and (silent) s. As they read, use the Phonic record sheet to note words that an individual misreads.

After reading 6 mins
- Turn to page 13.
- *Look at the picture of the Statue of Liberty's torch. What did Max and Ant say the torch looks like?* (Page 8 – Ant said it looked like an ice-cream cone and Max said it looked like a gherkin.) *What does it remind you of?*
- *Look back at page 11. Remember what happened in Invisible Threat when Tiger tried to fly the hot-air balloon. Who do you think is better at flying hot-air balloons: Max or Tiger?*
- Help children to find evidence to support their opinions. (E.g. on page 11 of *Statue Surprise*, Max manages to land near the statue's torch. Compare this with Tiger's performance on pages 16–17 of *Invisible Threat* when he tries to get the balloon under control, or when they have a bumpy landing on page 20.)

Takeaway: spelling 3 mins
- Explain that today's Takeaway is a spelling activity. Give each child PCM 84. They need to identify the tricky parts in each word (from *Invisible Threat* and *Statue Surprise*) and learn how to spell them using Look, Cover, Remember, Write, Check.

Statue Surprise

Purple band
Wonders of the World zone
Book 42

Resources
- CODE tracker files
- Wonders of the World zone Book 42 *Statue Surprise*
- Phonic record sheet – Purple band (page 28)
- PCM 85 Why did that happen?

Focus GPCs
gh as in ghostly, gu as in guess, mb as in thumb, (silent) s as in island

Team X words
Mini, watch

Exploring vocabulary (What does it mean?)
limb, numb

Additional, not yet decodable words
level, straight, towards, wrong, chameleon, moved, forward, warning, tongue, move, flared

Over the Edge

Introduction 4 mins
- Look at children's completed spelling challenges on PCM 84. (Takeaway from previous session.) Talk about the tricky parts in words and children's strategies for remembering them.
- If necessary, practise any words children found difficult using Look, Cover, Remember, Write, Check.
- *Can you remember where Max, Ant and Mini were at the end of the last story? (On the Statue of Liberty.)*

Before reading 4 mins
- *In the last session you practised the sounds you will need to use when you are reading today's story. Let's check that you can remember them as you read some words.*
- Turn to *Statue Surprise*, page 14.

Revise/Practise/Apply — **Word alert:** ghostly disguise numb island

What does it mean?
- *Before we read today's story, we will work together to understand the meanings of some of the words we will read today.*
- Read the words 'limb' and 'numb' and their definitions with the children and check they understand what they mean.

Reading the story 12 mins
- *Do you think Max, Ant and Mini will find the BITE?*
- *Rex is delivering a note about the BITE. Can you remember what it says? (It explains that the BITE is able to disguise itself and blend into the background.)*
- Turn to page 15 and read the title.
- *In this chapter, Max, Ant and Mini are searching for the BITE and getting more nervous as they explore the statue. Follow as I read and look out for any words that tell us how the characters are feeling and what sort of expression to use.*
- Pause at the end of the chapter and ask children if they spotted any words that tell them how the characters are feeling, e.g. 'nervously' (page 16) and 'urgently' (page 18).
- From Chapter 2, page 20, ask children to take turns reading a page each aloud. Pause at the end of page 27 and ask children to make predictions about what Ant might do next.
- Expect children to decode successfully, without being prompted. They should recognise the GPCs gh (/g/), gu (/g/), mb (/m/) and (silent) s. As they read, use the Phonic record sheet to note words that an individual misreads.
- If a child decodes a word incorrectly or is puzzled by a word, encourage them to read the whole word again, looking closely at the sounds in the word. They should then read the whole sentence again to check that it makes sense.

After reading 7 mins
- Turn to page 32.
- *Look back at the story. How does the author describe the BITE? Can you find some examples of words he chose?*
- Support children as they find descriptions in the story, e.g. 'terrible sight' (page 22); 'lashed out its tail' (page 24); 'flicking out its tongue', 'ghastly' (page 27); 'frightening', 'good at disguising itself' (page 31).
- *Read the split sentences describing what happened in the story. Can you summarise the action by joining the right pieces together using the word 'because'?*
- Ask children to take turns to read a completed sentence and check that it makes sense.

Takeaway: reading 3 mins
- Explain that today's Takeaway is a reading activity. Give each child PCM 85.
- *Join the parts of the sentences using the word 'because' to explain what happened as a result of each character's actions.*

Scare in the Air

Purple band
Wonders of the World zone
Book 43

Resources
- CODE tracker files
- Flashcards: gh, are, ear, ere, f, ff, ph
- Wonders of the World zone Book 43 *Scare in the Air*
- Words written on a flipchart or whiteboard: camouflage, phantom
- Phonic record sheet – Purple band (page 28)
- Challenge card only from **PCM 82 Cards and labels** for each child

Focus GPCs
gh as in rough, are as in aware, ear as in tearing, ere as in there

Team X word
Mini

Exploring vocabulary
camouflage, phantom

The Repti-BITE

Introduction 3 mins
- Look at children's joined sentences on PCM 85. (Takeaway from previous session.) Check that they all agree on how to match the sentences.
- Briefly discuss how Team X and Mini have met the Repti-BITE twice already and how they managed to escape.

Word workout and Before reading 6 mins
- *Let's do a short Word workout to get our reading and writing brains working.* (See pages 47–49 for details and an explanation of the flashcard activity and other Word workout activities. If any children still need to practise oral blending, select 2–3 words from a previous book.)

Revise/Practise — **Flashcards:** gh (/f/), are (/air/), ear (/air/), ere (/air/), f, ff, ph (/f/)

- *You already know the most common ways to spell the /f/ sound: 'f' as in 'fish', 'ff' as in 'puff' and 'ph' as in 'phone'. There is another way to spell /f/ that is found in a few words. It is 'gh' as in 'rough'.*
- *You also know that the most common way to spell the /air/ sound is 'air'. In some words it is spelled differently, for example, 'are' as in 'aware', 'ear' as in 'tearing', and 'ere' as in 'there'. Look out for this sound in today's story.*
- Turn to *Scare in the Air*, page 4.
- *Remember the sounds you have just practised and use them to blend the sounds and read the words.*

Apply — **Word alert:** rough beware tearing there

Reading the story 12 mins
- *What do Team X and Mini already know about the BITE?* (It can disguise itself like a real chameleon and doesn't like bright light or heat from the jet packs.)
- *What else do they need to know to help them defeat it?* (How to get the CODE key.)
- Show the words 'camouflage' and 'phantom'. Read them and check that children understand what they mean.
- *Camouflage means hiding by blending in with the background.*
- *A phantom is a ghost.*
- Turn to page 5 and ask children to take turns reading a page. Remind them to use their phonic knowledge as they decode unfamiliar words.
- Expect children to decode successfully, without being prompted. They should recognise the GPCs gh (/f/), are (/air/), ear (/air/) and ere (/air/). As they read, use the Phonic record sheet to note words that an individual misreads.

After reading 6 mins
- Turn to page 13.
- *Why will the CODE key be hard to find in this zone?*
- Refer children back to pages 10–11. Check they understand that the Gizmo can't give them the usual help to find the key and that Team X and Mini will have to find it themselves.
- *What do you think the author means when he describes how the Repti-BITE 'creeps up on its enemies like a phantom'?* (Page 8.) *Why do you think he chose these words?*
- Encourage children to make suggestions, providing ideas if necessary to help them understand the imagery, e.g. a phantom is silent, so the author is emphasising how dangerous and frightening this BITE is.

Takeaway: talking 3 mins
- *How does the Repti-BITE compare with the other BITEs? Look back through the books and zone logs to remind you of the other BITEs.*
- Give each child a challenge card from PCM 82. Ask them to talk to a partner and decide if this is the most frightening BITE that Team X and Mini have faced so far. They need to be able to give reasons for their answers.

Scare in the Air

Purple band
Wonders of the World zone
Book 43

Resources
- Wonders of the World zone Book 43 *Scare in the Air*
- Phonic record sheet – Purple band (page 28)
- CODE tracker files with **PCM 86 Missing words**

Focus GPCs
gh as in rough, are as in aware, ear as in tearing, ere as in there

Team X words
watch, Bee-machine

Exploring vocabulary (What does it mean?)
triumphantly, wreckage

Additional, not yet decodable words
we're, Eiffel, towards, could, move, sure, tongue, great, fuel, idea, wreckage

Rex Saves the Day

Introduction 4 mins
- Ask one child to give their opinion of the Repti-BITE (Takeaway from previous session) whilst the others listen and decide whether they agree or disagree. Can they back up their opinions using evidence from previous stories?
- *At the end of the last story, Max, Ant and Mini were trying to find the Repti-BITE, using Rex to pick up the trail. Where do you think they should look for it next?*
- Talk about the wonders that Team X and Mini have already explored and ask children what they can remember about them.

Before reading 4 mins
- *In the last session you practised the sounds you will need to use when you are reading today's story. Let's check that you can remember them as you read some words.*
- Turn to *Scare in the Air*, page 14.

| Revise/Practise/Apply | Word alert: enough   prepare   bear   where |

What does it mean?
- *Before we read today's story, we will work together to understand the meanings of some of the words we will read today.*
- Read the words 'triumphantly' and 'wreckage' and their definitions with the children and check they understand what they mean.

Reading the story 12 mins
- *Which wonder do you think Cat and Tiger will explore next?*
- *How do you think they will find the BITE if they can't see it?*
- Turn to page 15 and read the title and the first chapter aloud, demonstrating how to read fluently as children follow silently in their own books.
- From Chapter 2, page 18, ask children to take turns reading a page each.
- Expect children to decode successfully, without being prompted. They should recognise the GPCs gh (/f/), are (/air/), ear (/air/) and ere (/air/). As they read, use the Phonic record sheet to note words that an individual misreads.
- If a child decodes a word incorrectly or is puzzled by a word, encourage them to read the whole word again, looking closely at the sounds in the word. They should then read the whole sentence again to check that it makes sense.

After reading 7 mins
- Turn to page 32.
- *Look back at page 20 and read it again. Why did Tiger speak softly?*
- Encourage children to make suggestions. Offer help if needed, for example:
- *Tiger didn't want the BITE to know he was there. Cat and Tiger got caught by the BITE when they were in the Leaning Tower of Pisa and he didn't want it to happen again.*
- Turn back to page 32.
- *Rex was the hero of this story! Look at the pictures to remind you what happened, then explain how Rex saved Cat and Tiger.*

Takeaway: reading and writing 3 mins
- *Tiger used the Bee-machine in this story. What can you remember about what happened?*
- Give each child PCM 86.
- *Can you complete the sentences on this sheet, using the words to help you, and then write about where you would go if you could fly the Bee-machine yourself?*

Secret of the Stone

Purple band
Wonders of the World zone
Book 44

Resources
- CODE tracker files
- Flashcards: ei, eigh, aigh, ey, ay, ai, a, a-e
- Wonders of the World zone Book 44 *Secret of the Stone*
- Words written on a flipchart or whiteboard: conveyed, abseil
- Phonic record sheet – Purple band (page 28)
- PCM 87 Spelling challenge

Focus GPCs
ei as in veil, eigh as in eighty, aigh as in straight, ey as in they

Team X word
Mini

Exploring vocabulary
conveyed, abseil

Stop Team X!

Introduction 3 mins
- Look at children's ideas on PCM 86 about where they would fly in the Bee-machine. (Takeaway from previous session.)
- *At the end of the last story, Cat and Tiger's hot-air balloon crashed. How do you think they will travel around the Wonders of the World zone now?*

Word workout and Before reading 6 mins
- *Before we find out what happens to Team X and Mini next, we are going to do a short Word workout to get our reading and writing brains working.*
  (See pages 47–49 for details and an explanation of the flashcard activity and other Word workout activities. If any children still need to practise oral blending, select 2–3 words from a previous book.)

  Revise/Practise — **Flashcards:** ei (/ai/), eigh, aigh, ey (/ai/), ay, ai, a (/ai/), a-e

- *You already know the most common ways to spell /ai/: 'ay' as in 'day', 'ai' as in 'wait', 'a' as in 'baby' and 'a-e' as in 'take'. Other ways to spell /ai/ are 'ei' as in 'veil', 'eigh' as in 'eighty', 'aigh' as in 'straight' and 'ey' as in 'they'.*
- Turn to *Secret of the Stone*, page 4.
- *Remember the sound you have practised and use it to blend the sounds and read the words.*

  Apply — **Word alert:** unveil   eighty   straight   obey

Reading the story 12 mins
- *What can you remember about CODE?* (It's the computer that controls Micro World.)
- *How do you think CODE will try to stop Team X and Mini?*
- Show the words 'conveyed' and 'abseil'. Read them and check that the children understand what they mean.
- *If something is conveyed it is moved or passed on. For example, if you convey a message you pass it on to someone else.*
- *To abseil means that you slide down a rope, usually from somewhere high like the top of a mountain.*
- Turn to page 5 and read the title.
- Ask children to take turns reading a page each aloud. Remind them to use their phonic knowledge as they decode unfamiliar words.
- Expect children to decode successfully, without being prompted. They should recognise the GPCs ei (/ai/), eigh, aigh and ey (/ai/). As they read, use the Phonic record sheet to note words that an individual misreads.

After reading 6 mins
- Turn to page 13.
- *Max is abseiling into the stone circle because he thinks it is empty. Is he in danger? Why?*
- Check children understand that they, as readers, know more than Max does: that CODE has ordered the MITEs to march towards the stone circle.
- *Why do you think CODE called Team X "a major problem"?* (Page 5.)
- Encourage each child to contribute ideas, drawing on the stories they have read so far. Prompt if necessary, for example:
- *Team X and Mini keep defeating the BITEs and getting the keys. They only have a few more zones to visit and are getting closer to CODE.*
- *What do you think CODE's plan to protect the CODE key might be?*

Takeaway: spelling 3 mins
- Explain that today's Takeaway is a spelling activity. Give each child PCM 87. They need to identify the tricky parts in each word (from *Scare in the Air* and *Secret of the Stone*) and learn how to spell them using Look, Cover, Remember, Write, Check.

Secret of the Stone

Purple band
Wonders of the World zone
Book 44

Resources
- CODE tracker files
- Wonders of the World zone Book 44 *Secret of the Stone*
- Phonic record sheet – Purple band (page 28)
- Wonders of the World zone Books 41–43
- PCM 88 Wonders of the World CODE words
- Zone map (Book 41 *Invisible Threat*)
- PCM 81 Wonders of the World zone log

Focus GPCs
ei as in veil, eigh as in eighty, aigh as in straight, ey as in they

Team X words
Mini, watch

Exploring vocabulary (What does it mean?)
prey, veil

Additional, not yet decodable words
moving, movement, done, special, hero, wrong, weirdly, total, towards, directions

Surrounded

Introduction 4 mins
- Look at children's completed spelling challenges on PCM 87. (Takeaway from previous session.) Talk about the tricky parts in words and children's strategies for remembering them.
- Briefly ask children where Max, Ant and Mini were at the end of the last story. (At the stone circle.)

Before reading 4 mins
- 💬 *In the last session you practised the sound you will need to use when you are reading today's story. Let's check that you can remember it as you read some words.*
- Turn to *Secret of the Stone*, page 14.

Revise/Practise/Apply   **Word alert:** abseil   weight   straight   prey

What does it mean?
- 💬 *Before we read today's story, we will work together to understand the meanings of some of the words we will read.*
- Read the words 'prey' and 'veil' and their definitions with the children and check they understand what they mean.

Reading the story 12 mins
- 💬 *Mini thinks the CODE key might be hidden in the stone circle. Do you agree?*
- 💬 *We know that CODE has a plan. Do you think CODE will be able to trap Team X and Mini?*
- Turn to page 15 and read the title and the first chapter aloud as children follow silently in their books. Demonstrate how to read fluently and how to vary the pace, e.g. speeding up when describing an exciting piece of action (pages 17–18) and using different voices for characters (pages 19 and 21).
- 💬 *Did you notice how I changed the way I was reading in particular parts of the story? Try that too, to make your reading sound more exciting.*
- From Chapter 2, page 22, ask children to take turns reading a page each.
- Expect them to decode successfully, without being prompted. They should recognise the GPCs ei (/ai/), eigh, aigh and ey (/ai/). As they read, use the Phonic record sheet to note words that an individual misreads.
- If a child decodes a word incorrectly or is puzzled by a word, encourage them to read the whole word again, looking closely at the sounds in the word. They should then read the whole sentence again to check that it makes sense.

After reading 7 mins
- Turn to page 32.
- 💬 *Team X and Mini finally found the CODE key, but now it's up to us to help them by reading the special CODE words. These are invented words that we've never heard of before, but the computer needs them to open the exit door.*
- Ask children to work in pairs and explain in their own words what Max did to save Team X.
- They can then choose their favourite Wonders of the World book and reread it together.
- While children are working independently, work with each child individually as they read the list of invented CODE words (pseudo words). Check that they can recall the GPCs and blend them to read words. Keep a record using PCM 88.
- 💬 *Team X and Mini had a lucky escape that time and it sounds as though CODE is going to try even harder to stop them. Let's look at the zone map to see where Team X and Mini will be going next.*

Takeaway: reading and writing 3 mins
- Look together at PCM 81.
- 💬 *What needs to be completed to help you remember what happened in this zone?*
- Children take the log away to complete at school or at home. They can also take their favourite story away to share with someone.

81 Name _____ Date _____

Fill in the zone log.

Wonders of the World zone log

These are the dates when I read these books:

Invisible Threat *Statue Surprise* *Scare in the Air* *Secret of the Stone*

_____ _____ _____ _____

The BITE looked like this:

The best thing in this zone was:

_____

_____

Write three things Rex did to help the team.

1. _____

2. _____

3. _____

Purple band • Wonders of the World zone
Wonders of the World zone log
© Oxford University Press 2012. Copying permitted within the purchasing school only.

Children complete a reading record as they progress through the Wonders of the World zone.

82 Cards and labels

'Ask me about' labels

Ask me about the Leaning Tower of Pisa.

Ask me about the Leaning Tower of Pisa.

Ask me about the Leaning Tower of Pisa.

Ask me about the Leaning Tower of Pisa.

Challenge cards

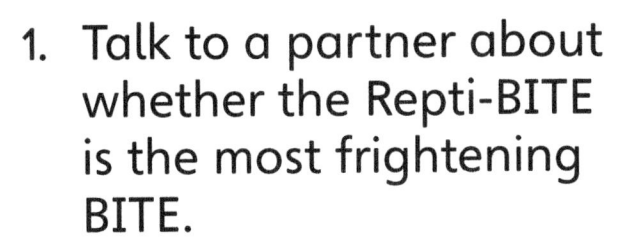

Talk about the BITEs.

1. Talk to a partner about whether the Repti-BITE is the most frightening BITE.
2. Use your zone logs and the books to remind you about the other BITEs.
3. Give reasons for your answer.

Talk about the BITEs.

1. Talk to a partner about whether the Repti-BITE is the most frightening BITE.
2. Use your zone logs and the books to remind you about the other BITEs.
3. Give reasons for your answer.

Purple band • Wonders of the World zone • **Cards and labels**
© Oxford University Press 2012. Copying permitted within the purchasing school only.

Children follow instructions on the cards to complete the activity.

Write a note

Finish Cat's note to Max, Ant and Mini.
Use the words to help you.

- chameleon
- invisible
- hide
- attack
- dangerous
- anywhere

Dear Max, Ant and Mini,

Look out! We have just seen the BITE and _____

From Cat

Spelling challenge

Follow the steps to spell the words.

1. Look at the word. Find the tricky part.
2. Cover the word. Say each sound. Write the word.
3. Check it is correct. ✓ or ✗
4. Write the word again.

Look	Write	Check	Write
cheered			
here			
interfere			
tier			
pier			
ghastly			
guide			
guess			
climb			
island			

Purple band ● Wonders of the World zone ● Spelling challenge

Children spell words from *Invisible Threat* and *Statue Surprise*.

Why did that happen?

Use **because** to join the two parts of the sentences.

{ because }

Rex delivered a note …	… the BITE trapped them.
Max, Ant and Mini climbed on to the statue's head …	… Ant aimed the heat from the jet pack at it.
Mini went flying into the air …	… Cat and Tiger needed to warn the others about the BITE.
Mini was saved …	… the BITE lashed out its tail.
The BITE veered away in terror …	… Max shot a wire from his watch.

Missing words

What is the Bee-machine like? Choose one word to complete each sentence.

Words to help you

The Bee-machine is so _____ it can fit on your hand.

- small
- heavy
- gigantic

You need to _____ to get in.

- grow
- curl up
- shrink

The Bee-machine can _____ like an insect.

- fly
- jump
- swim

Finish the sentence.

If I was flying the Bee-machine, I'd go _____

Purple band ● Wonders of the World zone ● **Missing words**

Children read the sentences, write the correct word in the gaps, then finish the last sentence.

Spelling challenge

Follow the steps to spell the words.

1. Look at the word. Find the tricky part.
2. Cover the word. Say each sound. Write the word.
3. Check it is correct. ✓ or ✗
4. Write the word again.

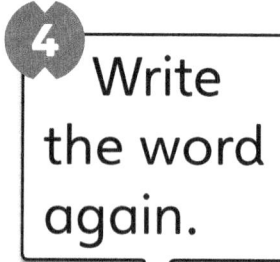

Look	Write	Check	Write
rough			
beware			
tearing			
there			
where			
unveil			
abseil			
eighty			
straight			
obey			

Wonders of the World CODE words

Help me read the CODE words.

plere	☐	cear	☐
jier	☐	reigs	☐
ghare	☐	bleigh	☐
gueer	☐	taight	☐
ghermb	☐	shey	☐

Into the Pyramid

Purple band
Pyramid Peril zone
Book 45

Resources
- CODE tracker files with **PCM 89 Pyramid Peril zone log**
- Zone map
- Pyramid Peril zone Book 45 *Into the Pyramid*
- Flashcards: ch, y
- Words written on a flipchart or whiteboard: brochure, chute
- Phonic record sheet – Purple band (page 28)
- Label only from **PCM 90 Cards and labels** for each child

Focus GPCs
ch as in brochure, ch as in anchor, y as in pyramid

Team X word
Mini

Exploring vocabulary
brochure, chute

Pyramid Peril

Introduction 3 mins
- If a child is new to CODE, give them their CODE tracker file. Explain that it's a special file to track Team X and Mini's progress through the Micro World zones. Ask them to complete PCM 3 (from *Teaching and Assessment Handbook 1*) as a cover sheet for their file.
- Give out PCM 89 and ask children to think about which details they need to note to make a record of this zone.
- Look at the zone map (on page 4 of *Into the Pyramid*) and follow the route that Team X and Mini have already taken. Point out that the Pyramid Peril zone is the final zone before they reach the centre of Micro World.

Word workout and Before reading 6 mins
💬 *Before we find out more about this zone, we will do a short Word workout to get our reading and writing brains working.*

(See pages 47–49 for details and an explanation of the flashcard activity and other Word workout activities. If any children still need to practise oral blending, select 2–3 words from a previous book.)

Revise/Practise Flashcards: ch (/sh/, /k/, /ch/), y (/i/)

💬 *You already know the most common way to pronounce 'ch': /ch/ as in 'church'. In some words, like 'brochure', it is pronounced /sh/. In others, like 'anchor', it is pronounced /k/.*

💬 *You already know the most common way to spell /i/ using the letter 'i'. In a few words we use the letter 'y', for example: 'pyramid'. You will be reading that word in today's story.*

- Turn to *Into the Pyramid*, page 5.

💬 *Remember the sounds you have just practised and use them to blend sounds and read the words.*

Apply Word alert: brochure   echo   school   Egypt

Reading the story 12 mins
💬 *What do you think the Pyramid Peril zone will be like?*
💬 *Do you know what pyramids were used for in ancient Egypt?*
- Encourage children to share what they know, filling in any gaps in their knowledge, e.g. pyramids were tombs built by the ancient Egyptians.
- Show the words 'brochure' and 'chute'. Read them and check that children know what they mean.
💬 *A brochure is a small book or magazine containing information.*
💬 *A chute is a sloping tube-like slide or passageway.*
- Turn to page 6 and ask children to take turns reading a page each. Remind them to use their phonic knowledge as they decode unfamiliar words.
- Expect children to decode successfully, without being prompted. They should recognise the GPCs ch (/sh/ and /k/) and y (/i/). As they read, use the Phonic record sheet to note any words that an individual misreads.

After reading 6 mins
- Turn to page 13.
💬 *Imagine you are on the Pyramid Peril ride. What can you hear, see, smell and touch? How do you feel?*
- Encourage children to scan the pages for information and use their imaginations. If necessary, demonstrate, for example:
💬 *The ride goes deep underground, so I think it would smell musty and damp.*
💬 *Do you think 'Pyramid Peril' is a good name for this zone? 'Peril' means danger. Have you spotted any dangers so far?*
- Support children in justifying their answers, using evidence from the text:
💬 *On page 10 it says there are secret passages and steep chutes, so that would make it feel dangerous.*

Takeaway: talking 3 mins
- Give each child a label from PCM 90. Challenge them to find out more about pyramids and then tell someone at school or home about them.

Into the Pyramid

Purple band
Pyramid Peril zone
Book 45

Resources
- Pyramid Peril zone Book 45 *Into the Pyramid*
- Phonic record sheet – Purple band (page 28)
- CODE tracker files with **PCM 91 Missing words**

Focus GPCs
ch as in brochure, ch as in anchor, y as in pyramid

Team X word
Mini

Exploring vocabulary (What does it mean?)
chariot, chaos

Additional, not yet decodable words
machine, should, great, seriously, several, towards, could, done

Into the Darkness

Introduction 4 mins
- Ask children what they found out about pyramids, e.g. where you can still see them today, what objects are found inside them. (Takeaway from previous session.)
- Would you like to visit the Pyramid Peril zone? How dangerous do you think it is in comparison to other zones that Team X and Mini have visited?

Before reading 4 mins
- In the last Word workout you practised sounds you will need to use when you are reading today's story. Let's check that you can remember them.
- Turn to *Into the Pyramid*, page 14.

Revise/Practise/Apply — **Word alert:** chute headache chaos pyramid

What does it mean?
- Before we read today's story, we will work together to understand the meanings of some of the words we will read today.
- Read the words 'chariot' and 'chaos' and their definitions with the children and check they understand what they mean.

Reading the story 12 mins
- We are going to read more about echoes today. Do you know what an echo sounds like? What sorts of places are good for making echoes? (E.g. caves or tunnels.)
- What would you expect to find inside a pyramid?
- Turn to page 15 and read the first chapter aloud as children follow silently in their books. Demonstrate how to use expression when reading about the echo on page 18.
- I'm going to read that page again to make it sound more like an echo. At first an echo is loud, then it gets fainter and fainter, so that's how I will read the repeated words.
- From Chapter 2, page 23, ask children to take turns reading a page each.
- Expect children to decode successfully, without being prompted. They should recognise the GPCs ch (/sh/ and /k/) and y (/i/). As they read, use the Phonic record sheet to note any words that an individual misreads.
- If a child decodes a word incorrectly, encourage them to read it again, looking closely at the individual sounds. Then ask them to read the whole sentence again to check that it makes sense.

After reading 7 mins
- Turn to page 32.
- How did Rex stop the cart? Can you finish the sentence?
- Support children in completing the sentence: 'Rex stopped the cart by …'
- Look back at page 30 and reread the phrase 'used his feet as anchors'. Check that children understand what it means.
- A ship's anchor wedges into the seabed to stop a ship from moving, just as Rex wedged his feet into the ground to stop the cart.
- Read page 19 again. How do you think Mini was feeling? Can you explain why Mini was annoyed with Cat?
- Draw out the idea that Mini was anxious because she wanted to find her dad and didn't want to waste time.
- Encourage children to draw parallels with their own experience, e.g. a sibling winding them up when they are worried about something.

Takeaway: reading and writing 3 mins
- Imagine you are going to make a warning sign about the traps inside the pyramids.
- Give each child PCM 91 and ask them to fill in the gaps to make a warning sign.

Another Way In

Purple band
Pyramid Peril zone
Book 46

Resources
- CODE tracker files
- Flashcards: ti, ci, ssi, sh, ch
- Pyramid Peril zone Book 46 *Another Way In*
- CODE launch story *The Adventure Begins*
- Words written on a flipchart or whiteboard: motion, vibrations
- Phonic record sheet – Purple band (page 28)
- PCM 92 Spelling challenge

Focus GPCs
ti as in direction, ci as in special, ssi as in mission

Exploring vocabulary
motion, vibrations

Rescue Mission

Introduction 3 mins
- Look at children's completed warning signs on PCM 91. (Takeaway from previous session.)
- Talk about what happened at the end of the last story. (Max, Cat, Mini and Rex were trapped in the pyramid.)

Word workout and Before reading 6 mins
🗨 *Let's do our Word workout to get our reading and writing brains working.*
(See pages 47–49 for details and an explanation of the flashcard activity and other Word workout activities. If any children still need to practise oral blending, select 2–3 words from a previous book.)

Revise/Practise **Flashcards:** ti (/sh/), ci (/sh/), ssi (/sh/), sh, ch (/sh/)

🗨 *You already know the most common way to spell /sh/ using the letters 'sh' and you have learned that it can sometimes be spelled 'ch' in words like 'brochure'. Here are some other ways to spell /sh/: 'ti' as in 'direction', 'ci' as in 'special' and 'ssi' as in 'mission'.*

- Turn to *Another Way In*, page 4.

🗨 *Remember the sound you have just practised and use it to blend the sounds and read the words.*

Apply **Word alert:** direction vibrations magician expression

Reading the story 12 mins
🗨 *How might Max, Cat, Mini and Rex escape from the pyramid?*
🗨 *Could Ant and Tiger use any of their kit to help the others?*
- Encourage children to suggest their own ideas, making use of what they know about Team X's watches and other kit. (If necessary, refer to *The Adventure Begins*, pages 15–17.)
- Show the words 'motion' and 'vibrations'. Read them and check that children understand what they mean.

🗨 *Motion means movement. If you set something in motion, you make it move.*
🗨 *Vibrations are when something shakes backwards and forwards rapidly.*

- Turn to page 5 and ask children to take turns reading a page each. Remind them to use their phonic knowledge as they decode unfamiliar words.
- Expect children to decode successfully, without being prompted. They should recognise the GPCs ti (/sh/), ci (/sh/) and ssi (/sh/). As they read, use the Phonic record sheet to note any words that an individual misreads.

After reading 6 mins
- Turn to page 13.

🗨 *Can you remember what caused the vibrations?*
- Help children understand the word 'cause', and to identify that the Driller was responsible for the vibrations.

🗨 *What effects did the vibrations have?*
- Help children to find evidence in the book: on page 11, everything shook; on page 12, something woke up.

🗨 *Read page 8 again. Why do you think Tiger said you'd need to be "a magician" to open the pyramid door?*
- Encourage children to discuss the choice of words, drawing out the fact that it's difficult to get through the door, so only magic could open it.

Takeaway: spelling 3 mins
- Explain that today's Takeaway is a spelling activity. Give each child PCM 92. They will need to identify the tricky parts in the words (from *Into the Pyramid* and *Another Way In*) and learn to spell them using Look, Cover, Remember, Write, Check.

Another Way In

Purple band
Pyramid Peril zone
Book 46

Resources
- CODE tracker files
- Pyramid Peril zone Book 46 *Another Way In*
- Phonic record sheet – Purple band (page 28)
- A set of cut-out boxes from **PCM 93 Shrink the story** for each child

Focus GPCs
ti as in direction, ci as in special, ssi as in mission

Team X words
Mini, watch

Exploring vocabulary (What does it mean?)
unravel, option

Additional, not yet decodable words
dinosaur, fossils, break, minute, moved, unravel, towards, wrapping, heights, especially, moving

Danger in the Dark

Introduction 4 mins
- Look at children's completed spelling challenges on PCM 92. (Takeaway from previous session.) Talk about the tricky parts in words and children's strategies for remembering them.
- *Which word was the hardest to spell? Which was the easiest?*
- If necessary, practise any words children found difficult using Look, Cover, Remember, Write, Check.

Before reading 4 mins
- *In the last Word workout you practised the sound you will need to use when you are reading today's story. Let's check that you can remember it.*
- Turn to *Another Way In*, page 14.

Revise/Practise/Apply	**Word alert:** action attention suspicion mission

What does it mean?
- *Before we read today's story, we will work together to understand the meanings of some of the words we will read today.*
- Read the words 'unravel' and 'option' and their definitions with the children and check they understand what they mean.

Reading the story 12 mins
- *Can you remember what Ant and Tiger are trying to do?* (Rescue the others from the pyramid.) *What are they using to help them?* (The Driller.)
- *What was disturbed at the end of the last story?* (A mummy.)
- Turn to page 15 and read the title.
- *In this chapter, things get more exciting. Listen carefully and see if you can hear the way I change my voice or speed up my reading to show that things are happening quickly.*
- Read the first chapter aloud as children follow silently in their books.
- Talk about how to use a loud, urgent voice to read Tiger's dialogue on pages 20–21 and ask children to try reading the speech themselves.
- From Chapter 2, page 22, ask children to take turns reading a page each.
- Expect children to decode successfully, without being prompted. They should recognise the GPCs ti (/sh/), ci (/sh/) and ssi (/sh/). As they read, use the Phonic record sheet to note any words that an individual misreads.
- If a child decodes a word incorrectly, encourage them to read it again, looking closely at the individual sounds. Then ask them to read the whole sentence again to check that it makes sense.

After reading 7 mins
- Turn to page 32.
- *What is the BITE's secret weapon?* (A third eye.) *How do you think it will use it to try to defeat Team X and Mini?*
- Encourage children to suggest ideas, recalling details from the story (e.g. using the eye to see where Ant and Tiger are hiding) and imagining other ways the eye could be used to defeat Team X and Mini.
- *Have a look at the three pictures of Ant and decide which word describes how he is feeling at each point in the story.*
- Help children read the three words and refer back to the relevant pages to see how Ant feels at each point. (Page 19: Ant looks interested in the mummy; page 20: he looks shocked because the mummy is attacking him; page 29: Ant looks terrified about climbing up the bandages.)
- *At the end of the story, Ant and Tiger start to think their mission is impossible. Do you agree?*

Takeaway: reading 3 mins
- Give each child a set of cut-out boxes from PCM 93 and a copy of *Another Way In*. They need to read the phrases summarising the story and decide which chapter each one is from and which order they should go in.
- *Read the story again to remind you what happens to Ant and Tiger in each chapter.*

Rock Shock

Purple band
Pyramid Peril zone
Book 47

Resources
- CODE tracker files
- Flashcards: si, s
- Pyramid Peril zone Book 47 *Rock Shock*
- Words written on a flipchart or whiteboard: lurks, intruders
- Phonic record sheet – Purple band (page 28)
- Challenge card only from **PCM 90 Cards and labels** for each child

Focus GPC
si as in vision

Team X word
Mini

Exploring vocabulary
lurks, intruders

The Mummy-BITE

Introduction 3 mins
- Look at children's completed sequencing activities from PCM 93. (Takeaway from the previous session.) Check that they all agree on the summaries for each chapter.

Word workout and Before reading 6 mins
- *Before we find out whether Ant and Tiger's mission really is impossible, let's do a Word workout to get our reading and writing brains working.*
  (See pages 47–49 for details and an explanation of the flashcard activity and other Word workout activities. If any children still need to practise oral blending, select 2–3 words from a previous book.)

  Revise/Practise Flashcards: si (/zh/), s (/zh/)

- *You already know one way to spell the sound /zh/ as in 'treasure', with an 's'. In some words, /zh/ is spelled 'si' as in 'vision'.*
- Turn to *Rock Shock*, page 4.
- *Remember the sound you have just practised and use it to blend the sounds and read the words.*

  Apply Word alert: decision vision treasures

Reading the story 12 mins
- *In the last story, Ant and Tiger found the BITE. What do you already know about the BITE?* (It's a mummy, it's wrapped in bandages, it can spray sand and bandages from its hands and it has a third eye.)
- *Can you remember how Max, Cat, Mini and Rex got trapped?* (They were in a cart but the door closed before they could make it out.)
- Show the words 'lurks' and 'intruders'. Read them and check children understand what they mean.
- *If you lurk somewhere, it means you wait in hiding.*
- *Intruders are uninvited visitors.*
- Turn to page 5 and ask children to take turns reading a page each. Remind them to use their phonic knowledge as they decode unfamiliar words.
- Expect children to decode successfully, without being prompted. They should recognise the GPC si (/zh/). As they read, use the Phonic record sheet to note any words that an individual misreads.

After reading 6 mins
- Turn to page 13.
- *Now that you have read about the Mummy-BITE, can you summarise the most important information about how it attacks? What three things can it do when it is in attack mode?* (It can shoot bandages, use its third eye to see round corners and into dark shadows, and spray sand.)
- *Can you finish the sentence using the words provided?*
- Help children work out the answer:
- **The Gizmo says** the BITE lurks deep inside the pyramid **but** it has left the pyramid **so** Max, Cat and Mini have to leave the pyramid to find the BITE.

Takeaway: talking 3 mins
- Give each child a challenge card from PCM 90 and a copy of *Rock Shock*.
- *How are Max, Cat and Mini feeling at the end of today's story? Work with a partner to practise reading pages 10–12 again, showing how each character is feeling by changing your voice. You could even add a sound effect for the echo they hear! When you are ready, perform it to someone else.*

Rock Shock
Purple band
Pyramid Peril zone
Book 47

Resources
- Pyramid Peril zone Book 47 *Rock Shock*
- Phonic record sheet – Purple band (page 28)
- CODE tracker files with PCM 94 Questions and answers

Focus GPC
si as in vision

Team X words
Mini, watch

Exploring vocabulary (What does it mean?)
confusion, hurtling

Additional, not yet decodable words
forward, towards, halt, oh, could, minute, tunnel, should

Don't Look Back!

Introduction 4 mins
- Listen to pairs of children performing their reading from the previous session's Takeaway. Talk about the most effective ways to use their voices to show the characters' feelings.
- Ask children to recall where Team X and Mini are at this point. If necessary, remind them that they have split into two groups.

Before reading 4 mins
- *In the last Word workout you practised the sound you will need to use when you are reading today's story. Let's check that you can remember it.*
- Turn to *Rock Shock*, page 14.

Revise/Practise/Apply — **Word alert:** explosion   confusion   measure

What does it mean?
- *Before we read today's story, we will work together to understand the meanings of some of the words we will read today.*
- Read the words 'confusion' and 'hurtling' and their definitions with the children and check they understand what they mean.

Reading the story 12 mins
- *What have Max, Cat and Mini decided to do?* (Search for the Mummy-BITE inside the pyramid.)
- *Do you know what ancient Egyptian writing was like? In this story, Max, Cat and Mini will need to work out a message written on the wall. Look out for the tiny Egyptian pictures.*
- Turn to page 15 and read the title.
- Read the first chapter aloud as children follow silently in their books. Pause at the end of page 21 and check whether children noticed the use of capitals in the word 'STOP'. Talk about why the author chose to write it that way. (I.e. for emphasis, to show how loud Cat's voice was.)
- From Chapter 2, page 22, ask children to take turns reading a page each.
- Expect children to decode successfully, without being prompted. They should recognise the GPC si (/zh/). As they read, use the Phonic record sheet to note any words that an individual misreads.
- If a child decodes a word incorrectly, encourage them to read it again, looking closely at the individual sounds. Then ask them to read the whole sentence again to check that it makes sense.

After reading 7 mins
- Turn to page 32.
- *What was the trap in this story? What or who do you think set it off?*
- Check that children can explain the trap in their own words and give their own opinion about what set this one off.
- *Look at the picture of Max, Cat and Mini swinging over the pit. How do you think they are feeling? Choose a character and describe what they might say, think and feel.*
- Give children time to think about their answers. Make notes to record what they say about different characters, e.g. Mini might say, "I'm so scared. Please don't let me fall." She might be thinking that the wire will not hold them all, and she is probably feeling terrified.

Takeaway: reading and writing 3 mins
- Explain that today's Takeaway is a reading and writing activity. Give each child PCM 94 and a copy of *Rock Shock*. They need to summarise the story by reading the questions and writing answers to them.
- *If you're not sure of the answers, look back through the story to remind you.*

Hang On!
Purple band
Pyramid Peril zone
Book 48

Resources
- CODE tracker files
- Flashcards: el, il, al, le
- Pyramid Peril zone Book 48 *Hang On!*
- Phonic record sheet – Purple band (page 28)
- Flipchart or whiteboard
- PCM 95 Spelling challenge

Focus GPCs
el as in travel, il as in pupil, al as in animal

Exploring vocabulary
survival

Uncovered

Introduction 3 mins
- Look at children's completed answers on PCM 94. (Takeaway from previous session.) Use their answers to summarise and review the story.

Word workout and Before reading 6 mins
- *Let's do a short Word workout to get our reading and writing brains working before we read today's story.*
  (See pages 47–49 for details and an explanation of the flashcard activity and other Word workout activities. If any children still need to practise oral blending, select 2–3 words from a previous book.)

  Revise/Practise Flashcards: el (/ul/), il (/ul/), al (/ul/), le (/ul/)

- *You already know the most common way to spell /ul/ at the end of a word: 'le' as in 'table'. We are going to look at three more ways to spell /ul/: 'el' as in 'travel', 'il' as in 'pupil' and 'al' as in 'animal'.*
- Turn to *Hang On!*, page 4.
- *Remember the sound you have just practised and use it to blend the sounds and read the words.*

  Apply Word alert: travel   peril   survival

Reading the story 12 mins
- *Where were Ant and Tiger when you last saw them?* (Clinging on to the Mummy-BITE's bandages.)
- *Can you remember where the CODE key is?* (On the Mummy-BITE's arm.) *How do you think Team X and Mini will get the CODE key?*
- Look at the word 'survival'. Read it and check that children understand what it means (staying alive).
- Turn to page 5 and ask children to take turns reading a page each. Remind them to use their phonic knowledge as they decode unfamiliar words.
- Expect children to decode successfully, without being prompted. They should recognise the GPCs el (/ul/), il (/ul/) and al (/ul/). As they read, use the Phonic record sheet to note any words that an individual misreads.

After reading 6 mins
- Turn to page 13.
- *How did the Mummy-BITE realise that Ant and Tiger were on its body?*
- Look at the two pictures to help children remember what happened, then challenge them to compose a sentence,
  e.g. **At first** the BITE thought they were an itch and tried to scratch them, **but then** the BITE saw them with its third eye.
- *There is lots of excitement in this story. How can you make it sound exciting when you are reading aloud?*
- Support children in coming up with some tips, e.g. by reading quickly, loudly, or adding expression to show how a character is feeling. Write their ideas on a flipchart or whiteboard.
- *Let's read pages 8–12 again and see if we can use these tips to help us.*
- Help children to see where they could put their tips into practise, e.g. page 8: increasing the pace of reading to show that events happened very fast; page 9: reading 'SWAT!' loudly; page 11: making Tiger's exclamation sound terrified.
- *Do you think Ant and Tiger will escape from the BITE by jumping on the camel's back?*

Takeaway: spelling 3 mins
- Explain that today's Takeaway is a spelling activity. Give each child PCM 95. They need to identify the tricky parts in the words (from *Rock Shock* and *Hang On!*) and learn to spell them using Look, Cover, Remember, Write, Check.

Hang On!
Purple band
Pyramid Peril zone
Book 48

Resources
- CODE tracker files
- Pyramid Peril zone Book 48 *Hang On!*
- Phonic record sheet – Purple band (page 28)
- Pyramid Peril zone Books 45–47
- PCM 96 Pyramid Peril CODE words
- PCM 89 Pyramid Peril zone log

Focus GPCs
el as in travel, il as in pupil, al as in animal

Team X words
watch, Mini

Exploring vocabulary (What does it mean?)
reins, skittles

Additional, not yet decodable words
either, should, could, wanted, great, towards, opposite, hey

A Bumpy Ride

Introduction 4 mins
- Look at children's completed spelling challenges on PCM 95. (Takeaway from previous session.) Talk about the tricky parts in words and children's strategies for remembering them.
- *Do you think Ant and Tiger will be able to get the CODE key?*

Before reading 4 mins
- *In the last Word workout you practised the sound you will need to use when you are reading today's story. Let's check that you can remember it.*
- Turn to *Hang On!*, page 14.

Revise/Practise/Apply — Word alert: camel pupil animal final

What does it mean?
- *Before we read today's story, we will work together to understand the meanings of some of the words we will read today.*
- Read the words 'reins' and 'skittles' and their definitions with the children and check they understand what they mean.

Reading the story 12 mins
- *How did Ant and Tiger escape from the Mummy-BITE?* (By jumping on a camel.)
- *What do you think it would be like to ride on a camel?*
- Turn to page 15 and explain that you are going to read the first chapter aloud as children follow silently in their books.
- *At the end of this chapter, I'm going to tell you what I think of it and I'd like to hear what you think, too.*
- Pause at the end of page 19 and demonstrate how to give an opinion, using evidence from the text. For example:
- *I thought this chapter was good because it had details about what it would really be like to ride on a camel, such as bouncing up and down (page 15), putting up with the camel's bellowing and bad breath (page 18) and running really fast (page 19). What do you think?*
- From Chapter 2, page 20, ask children to take turns reading a page each.
- Expect children to decode successfully, without being prompted. They should recognise the GPCs el (/ul/), il (/ul/) and al (/ul/). As they read, use the Phonic record sheet to note any words that an individual misreads.
- If a child decodes a word incorrectly, encourage them to read it again, looking closely at the individual sounds. Then ask them to read the whole sentence again to check that it makes sense.

After reading 7 mins
- Turn to page 32 and tell children they need to help Team X and Mini by reading the invented CODE words.
- Ask children to work in pairs and explain how Ant and Tiger got the CODE key. They can then choose their favourite Pyramid Peril book and reread it together.
- While the pairs are working independently, work with each child individually as they read the list of invented CODE words (pseudo words). Check they can recall the GPCs and blend them to read words. Keep a record using PCM 96.
- *Team X and Mini have managed to get through all the zones. Do you think they will find Marvel and stop CODE? Did you notice the final words in today's story: 'Team X went to put the CODE key into what they thought was the final door …'. That sounds a bit worrying. What do you think will happen next?*

Takeaway: reading and writing 3 mins
- Look together at PCM 89.
- *What needs to be completed to help you remember what happened in this zone?*
- Children can complete their log at school or at home. They can also take their favourite story away to share with someone.

89 Name _____ Date _____

Fill in the zone log.

Pyramid Peril zone log

These are the dates when I read these books:

Into the Pyramid | *Another Way In* | *Rock Shock* | *Hang On!*

_____ _____ _____ _____

The BITE looked like this:

How scary was the BITE? — terrifying (5) / cute (0)

The best thing in the Pyramid Peril zone was:

_____

Write three things Ant and Tiger did in this zone.

1. _____

2. _____

3. _____

Purple band ● Pyramid Peril zone ● **Pyramid Peril zone log**

Children complete a reading record as they progress through the Pyramid Peril zone.

90 Cards and labels

'Ask me about' labels

Ask me about the pyramids.

Ask me about the pyramids.

Ask me about the pyramids.

Ask me about the pyramids.

Challenge cards

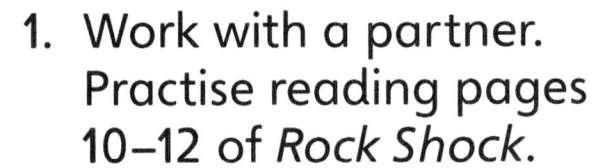

Read Max, Cat and Mini's speech.

1. Work with a partner. Practise reading pages 10–12 of *Rock Shock*.
2. Change your voice to show how each character is feeling.
3. When you are ready, perform your reading to someone else.

Read Max, Cat and Mini's speech.

1. Work with a partner. Practise reading pages 10–12 of *Rock Shock*.
2. Change your voice to show how each character is feeling.
3. When you are ready, perform your reading to someone else.

Purple band ● Pyramid Peril zone ● **Cards and labels**
© Oxford University Press 2012. Copying permitted within the purchasing school only.

Children follow instructions on the cards to complete the activity.

Missing words

Fill in the gaps using the words.

- they will chase you
- Enter at your peril!
- Beware of sand
- traps

1. Danger! _____

2. Look out for _____.

3. Beware of beetles because _____ _____.

4. _____ because it will fill the chamber.

Spelling challenge

Follow the steps to spell the words.

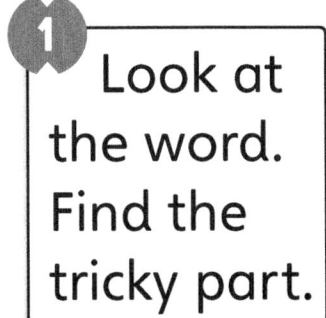

1. Look at the word. Find the tricky part.
2. Cover the word. Say each sound. Write the word.
3. Check it is correct. ✓ or ✗
4. Write the word again.

Look	Write	Check	Write
brochure			
echo			
headache			
pyramid			
Egypt			
direction			
magician			
suspicion			
mission			
expression			

Shrink the story

 In Chapter 1, Ant and Tiger …	 In Chapter 2, Ant and Tiger …	 In Chapter 3, Ant and Tiger …
… used the Driller.	… ran away from the BITE.	… climbed the BITE's bandages.
… saw dinosaur fossils.	… saw the BITE's third eye.	… tried to edge towards the CODE key.
… found the BITE.	… used their watches to shrink.	… started to think their mission was impossible.

Purple band • Pyramid Peril zone • **Shrink the story**

Cut out the boxes. Children order the phrases to summarise each chapter in the story.

94 Name _____ Date _____

Questions and answers

Read the questions and write answers to them.

In Chapter 1: Who was looking in the pyramid?
_____

What came hurtling down the passage? _____
_____

Why did Cat yell "STOP!"? _____
_____

In Chapter 2: How did Max, Cat and Mini get across the pit? _____
_____

In Chapter 3: Where was the doorway to the secret passage? _____
_____

What was outside the pyramid? _____

Name _____ **Date** _____

Spelling challenge

Follow the steps to spell the words.

1 Look at the word. Find the tricky part.

2 Cover the word. Say each sound. Write the word.

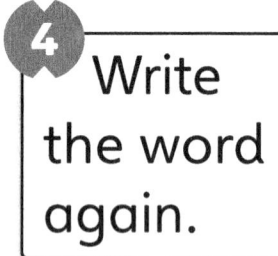

3 Check it is correct. ✓ or ✗

4 Write the word again.

Look	Write	Check	Write
decision			
vision			
confusion			
treasure			
measure			
travel			
pupil			
peril			
survival			
normal			

Purple band • Pyramid Peril zone • Spelling challenge
© Oxford University Press 2012. Copying permitted within the purchasing school only.

Children spell words from *Rock Shock* and *Hang On!*

Pyramid Peril CODE words

Help me read the CODE words.

jochure	☐	crission	☐
echorm	☐	drision	☐
shoficial	☐	broval	☐
jation	☐	napil	☐

A Shock for Mini

Gold band
Marvel Towers zone
Book 49

Resources
- Zone map
- Marvel Towers zone Book 49 *A Shock for Mini*
- Phonic record sheet – Gold band (page 29)
- Challenge card only from **PCM 97 Cards and labels** for each child
- CODE tracker files

Focus GPC
oul as in could

Team X word
Mini

Exploring vocabulary (What does it mean?)
fizzing

Our Adventures So Far

Introduction 3 mins
- If a child is new to CODE, give them their CODE tracker file. Explain that it's a special file to track Team X and Mini's progress through the Micro World zones. Ask them to complete PCM 3 (from *Teaching and Assessment Handbook 1*) as a cover sheet for their file.
- Look at the zone map (on page 4 of *A Shock for Mini*) and use it to recap the story of Team X and Mini's movement through the zones. Point out that Marvel Towers is at the centre of Micro World.
- *Team X and Mini have been through all the zones and collected 12 CODE keys, so they are very close to completing their mission. What have they still got to do? How do you think they are feeling now?*

Word workout and Before reading 5 mins
- *Let's do a Word workout to get our reading and writing brains working.* (See pages 47–49 for details and an explanation of the additional Word workout activities. If any children still need to practise oral blending, select 2–3 words from a previous book.)
- Turn to *A Shock for Mini*, page 5.

Revise/Practise/Apply **Word alert:** could would soon room chewed

- *You already know the most common ways to spell the short /oo/ sound. Look at the words 'could' and 'would'. Which letters spell the short /oo/ sound in these words?* ('oul'.) *Look out for these words when you are reading today.*
- *You already know there are different ways to spell the long /oo/ sound. Look at the words 'soon', 'room' and 'chewed'. Which letters make the long /oo/ sound in these words?* (S**oo**n, r**oo**m, ch**ew**ed.)

What does it mean?
- *Before we read today's story, we will work together to understand the meaning of one of the words we will read today.*
- Read the word 'fizzing' and its definition with the children and check they understand what it means.

Reading the story 12 mins
- *Why is Mini determined to get into Marvel Towers?* (To rescue her dad.)
- *Can you remember what happened to Macro Marvel on the opening day of Micro World?* (He went into the Shrinker, then sent Mini a message telling her to stop CODE.)
- Turn to page 6 and ask children to take turns reading a page each. Check they understand that pages 7–11 are a summary of Mini's adventures.
- Expect children to decode successfully, without being prompted. They should recognise the GPC oul (short /oo/). As they read, use the Phonic record sheet to note any words that an individual misreads.
- Check that, after they decode and if the need arises, children reread a sentence to check that it makes sense, self-correcting if necessary.

After reading 7 mins
- Turn to page 13.
- *What were the most important events in Mini's Micro World adventures? What would you add to Mini's notes?*
- *How was Mini feeling when she was making notes?*
- Give children time to find evidence in the story, e.g. page 7: 'My stomach is fizzing with nerves'; page 11: 'The giant eye … gives me the creeps'; page 12: "How can I sleep at a time like this?".
- *What do you think Mini will do next?*
- Ask children to choose one of the three options, giving their reasons.

Takeaway: talking 3 mins
- Give each child a challenge card from PCM 97. Challenge them to talk to a partner about Micro World, discussing their favourite zones and rides, and which BITEs they found the most frightening. They can refer back to their CODE tracker files to remind them.

A Shock for Mini

Gold band
Marvel Towers zone
Book 49

Resources
- Marvel Towers zone Book 49 *A Shock for Mini*
- Phonic record sheet – Gold band (page 29)
- CODE tracker files with PCM 98 Reading log: A Shock for Mini

Focus GPC
oul as in could

Team X word
Mini

Exploring vocabulary (What does it mean?)
nano

Additional, not yet decodable words
two, wrong, move, gone, towards, warning, suit

One Step Closer

Introduction and Before reading 4 mins

- Ask children which zones and rides they like the best and which BITE they think is the most frightening. (Takeaway from previous session.)
- *Before we read, we will do some activities to get us ready for the next story.*
- Turn to *A Shock for Mini*, page 14.

Revise/Practise/Apply	**Word alert:** should stool blue intrude flew control

- Ask children to take turns to choose a word, say the sounds, then blend the sounds to read the word. Check they can recall the focus GPC.

What does it mean?
- *Before we read today's story, we will work together to understand the meaning of one of the words we will read today.*
- Read the word 'nano' and its definition with the children and check they understand what it means.

Guided/group reading 16 mins

- *What do you think has happened to Macro Marvel?*
- *Do you think it will be easy to rescue Macro Marvel?*
- Turn to page 15 and read the first chapter aloud as children follow silently in their books. Demonstrate how to use appropriate expression for speech, e.g. using a cold, hard voice when Marvel speaks on pages 20–21.
- Pause at the end of Chapter 1.
- *Did Mini do what you expected her to? Why did she get such a shock when she saw her dad?*
- From Chapter 2, page 23, ask children to continue reading the book quietly at their own pace. Listen to each individual reader in turn.
- Expect children to decode successfully, without being prompted. They should recognise the GPC oul (short /oo/). As they read, use the Phonic record sheet to note any words that an individual misreads.
- If a child decodes a word incorrectly, encourage them to read it again, looking closely at the individual sounds. Then ask them to read the whole sentence again to check that it makes sense.

After reading 7 mins

- When each child has finished reading, ask them to turn to page 32 and explain that they need to think of one sentence to summarise each chapter. When all the children have finished reading, listen to some of their sentences.
- *How do Mini's feelings change during the story? Look at the pictures on page 32, decide how frightened Mini is in each one, and give her a rating using the 0–5 scale.*
- Ask each child to take on the role of a Team X character. Reread pages 27–31 with children reading the speech while you act as narrator. Encourage them to use the appropriate expression for that character.
- *Did the story surprise you? Do you think Team X will manage to get inside Marvel's body?*

Takeaway: reading and writing 3 mins

- *While you are reading the Marvel Towers' stories, you are going to start completing your own reading log. It is like a diary where you write down your thoughts and questions about what you have read.*
- Give each child PCM 98 and a copy of *A Shock for Mini* to take away.

A BITE Inside

Gold band
Marvel Towers zone
Book 50

Resources
- CODE tracker files
- Marvel Towers zone Book 50 *A BITE Inside*
- Phonic record sheet – Gold band (page 29)
- PCM 99 Spelling challenge

Focus GPCs
wr as in wrist, rh as in rhythm

Team X words
Mini, watch

Exploring vocabulary (What does it mean?)
brow

A Micro Plan

Introduction 3 mins
- Look at children's completed reading logs (Takeaway from previous session) and ask them to share their ideas about the most important event in the previous story.

Word workout and Before reading 6 mins
- *Let's do a Word workout to get our reading and writing brains working.* (See pages 47–49 for details and an explanation of the additional Word workout activities. If any children still need to practise oral blending, select 2–3 words from a previous book.)
- Turn to *A BITE Inside*, page 4.

Revise/Practise/Apply	Word alert: wrist rhythm wrinkling rhubarb rose

- *You already know the most common way to spell /r/ using the letter 'r'. We are going to look at two more ways to spell /r/: 'wr' as in 'wrist' and 'rh' as in 'rhythm'.*
- Look at the words and ask children to identify the tricky parts.
- Look at the words 'wrinkling', 'rhubarb' and 'rose'. Ask children to take turns to choose a word, say the sounds and then blend the sounds to read the word. Check that they remember the focus GPCs wr and rh.

What does it mean?
- *Before we read today's story, we will work together to understand the meaning of one of the words we will read today.*
- Read the word 'brow' and its definition with the children and check they understand what it means. Ask children to point to their foreheads.

Reading the story 12 mins
- *Team X have special crafts that they use to get around. What do you know about Hawkwing?*
- *What does an X-ray show you? How could Team X and Mini use one to help them?*
- Turn to page 5 and ask children to take turns reading a page each.
- Expect children to decode successfully, without being prompted. They should recognise the GPCs wr (/r/) and rh (/r/). As they read, use the Phonic record sheet to note any words that an individual misreads.
- Check that, after they decode and if the need arises, children reread a sentence to check that it makes sense, self-correcting if necessary.

After reading 6 mins
- Turn to page 13.
- *Look back at page 7. It says that Macro Marvel laughed 'madly'. What does this tell you about him?* (It is evidence that he is being controlled by CODE.) *Try using a different word to describe how he laughed. How does that change the meaning?*
- Help children understand the impact of using different vocabulary by rereading the sentence and inserting a new word, e.g. 'happily' or 'quietly' instead of 'madly'. Discuss how the author used the word 'madly' to make the point about Marvel being under CODE's control.
- *Imagine you are with Team X and are flying into Marvel's mouth. What do you think it would be like?*
- *Can you remember what Cat said about the plan? What did she think of it? How did she feel?*

Takeaway: spelling 3 mins
- Explain that today's Takeaway is a spelling activity. Give each child PCM 99. They will need to identify the tricky parts in the words (from *A Shock for Mini* and *A BITE Inside*) and learn to spell them using Look, Cover, Remember, Write, Check.

A BITE Inside

Gold band
Marvel Towers zone
Book 50

Mini Fights Back

Introduction and Before reading 4 mins

- Look at children's completed spelling challenges on PCM 99. (Takeaway from previous session.) Talk about the tricky parts in words and children's strategies for remembering them.
- 💬 *Before we read, we will do some activities to get us ready for the next story.*
- Turn to *A BITE Inside*, page 14.

Revise/Practise/Apply	**Word alert:** wrong wriggle wrestle rhythm

- Ask children to take turns to choose a word, say the sounds and then blend the sounds to read the word. Check that they can recall the focus GPCs.

What does it mean?
- 💬 *Before we read today's story, we will work together to understand the meanings of some of the words we will read today.*
- Read the words 'gradually' and 'fire extinguishers' and their definitions with the children and check that they understand what they mean.

Guided/group reading 16 mins

- 💬 *Can you remember where Mini and Rex are? How did they get trapped?* (They were captured by MITEs in the Control Room.)
- 💬 *Does Mini know what is wrong with her dad?* (No.)
- Turn to page 15 and read the first chapter aloud as children follow silently in their books. Demonstrate how to make inferences, for example:
- 💬 *I can tell that Mini is feeling very confused because her dad isn't behaving like he normally does. On page 15, she asks what is wrong because she's never seen him like this; on page 17, it says that she was shocked.*
- From Chapter 2, page 22, ask children to continue reading the book quietly at their own pace. Listen in on each individual reader in turn.
- Expect children to decode successfully, without being prompted. They should recognise the GPCs wr (/r/) and rh (/r/). As they read, use the Phonic record sheet to note any words that an individual misreads.
- If a child decodes a word incorrectly, encourage them to read it again, looking closely at the individual sounds. Then ask them to read the whole sentence again to check that it makes sense.

After reading 7 mins

- When each child has finished reading the story, ask them to turn to page 32 and think about the three things Rex did to help Mini escape.
- When all children have finished reading, ask a child to retell 'Rex's story', using the pictures to help them remember what happened.
- 💬 *Now read the sentences about the story and decide which ones are true and which are false. Can you find evidence in the story to explain your answers?*
- Help children find evidence in the story for each answer, e.g. page 15: Mini had never heard her dad use such a cold voice – this shows he is usually friendly; page 26: the MITEs soon got back up after slipping over and, on page 30, they tried to wrestle the Gizmo away from Mini – showing that they don't give up easily; page 28: Mini had inherited her dad's good memory.
- 💬 *Why do you think Mini was so desperate to get her Gizmo back?*
- Encourage children to think about what she uses it for, using evidence from previous stories, e.g. she uses it to find information to help them defeat the BITEs, and she uses it to make notes about her adventures.

Takeaway: reading and writing 3 mins

- 💬 *You are going to record your ideas about the book you have just finished on your reading log. There are some questions to get you thinking.*
- Give each child PCM 100 and a copy of *A BITE Inside* to take away.

Resources
- CODE tracker files
- Marvel Towers zone Book 50 *A BITE Inside*
- Phonic record sheet – Gold band (page 29)
- PCM 100 Reading log: A BITE Inside

Focus GPCs
wr as in wrist, rh as in rhythm

Team X word
Mini

Exploring vocabulary (What does it mean?)
gradually, fire extinguishers

Additional, not yet decodable words
swallowed, answer, question, gone, towards, extinguishers, done, fortunately, two, moved, circuits

Mission Marvel

Gold band
Marvel Towers zone
Book 51

Resources
- CODE tracker files
- Marvel Towers zone Book 51 *Mission Marvel*
- Phonic record sheet – Gold band (page 29)
- Label only from **PCM 97** Cards and labels for each child

Focus GPC
wh as in whole

Team X word
Mini

Exploring vocabulary (What does it mean?)
pincers

The Virus-BITE

Introduction 3 mins
- Look at children's completed reading logs on PCM 100 (Takeaway from previous session) and share their ideas about what message Mini might send to Team X.

Word workout and Before reading 6 mins
- *Before we find out more about the BITE, we will do a Word workout to get our reading and writing brains working.*
  (See pages 47–49 for details and an explanation of the additional Word workout activities. If any children still need to practise oral blending, select 2–3 words from a previous book.)
- Turn to *Mission Marvel*, page 4.

  Revise/Practise/Apply Word alert: whole hopēd hidden

- *The most common way to spell /h/ is using the letter 'h'. In some words we spell it 'wh' as in 'whole'. Find the tricky part in the word 'whole'.*
- Look at the words 'whole', 'hoped' and 'hidden'. Ask children to take turns to choose a word, say the sounds and then blend the sounds to read the word. Check that they remember the focus GPC.

What does it mean?
- *Before we read today's story, we will work together to understand the meaning of one of the words we will read today.*
- Read the word 'pincers' and its definition with the children and check they understand what it means.

Reading the story 12 mins
- *Why is Macro Marvel feeling unwell?* (Because there's a BITE inside of him.) *What signs of illness have we read about?* (Running nose, shivering, sneezing, tiredness.)
- *How would Mini usually find out about a BITE?* (Draw out the idea that there is a potential problem. She usually uses her Gizmo, but this is a new BITE that they didn't know about so it's not on her Gizmo.)
- Turn to page 5 and ask children to take turns reading a page each.
- Expect children to decode successfully, without being prompted. They should recognise the GPC wh (/h/). As they read, use the Phonic record sheet to note any words that an individual misreads.
- Check that, after they decode and if the need arises, children reread a sentence to check that it makes sense, self-correcting if necessary.
- *Did anything puzzle or surprise you in that story?*

After reading 6 mins
- Turn to page 13.
- *Look back at the computer pages about the Virus-BITE on pages 8–10. Compare them to the Gizmo pages containing information about the BITEs. Did you notice any differences?* (E.g. The computer pages are written by CODE; 'CODE files' appears at the top of each page; they include details of CODE's plan.)
- *Listen to this statement: 'CODE is trying to keep the Virus-BITE secret.' Can you find two pieces of evidence from the story to prove this?*
- Help children to look back to specific pages to locate evidence, e.g. pages 8–10: the 'Locked' heading; page 10: 'the CODE key will be hidden forever'.
- *At the end of the story, Mini sent a message to Max about the Virus-BITE. What do you think it said?*
- Encourage children to look back through the story to find useful information about the BITE that Mini could pass on to Team X.

Takeaway: talking 3 mins
- *What do you think Team X will see inside Macro Marvel's body?*
- Give each child a label from PCM 97. Challenge them to find out about the human body, particularly the position of the heart, lungs and stomach, and tell someone at school or home what they have discovered.

Mission Marvel

Gold band
Marvel Towers zone
Book 51

Resources
- Marvel Towers zone Book 51 *Mission Marvel*
- Phonic record sheet – Gold band (page 29)
- CODE tracker files with **PCM 101 Reading log: Mission Marvel**

Focus GPC
wh as in whole

Team X words
watch, Mini

Exploring vocabulary (What does it mean?)
throttle, jutting out

Additional, not yet decodable words
heart, heartbeat, move, two, engines, towards, great, halt, upwards, coughing, swallowed

The Chase

Introduction and Before reading 4 mins

- Ask children what they found out about the inside of the body. (Takeaway from previous session.) Can they indicate where their heart, lungs and stomach are?
- Before we find out what happens next to Team X and Mini, we will do some activities to get us ready to read.
- Turn to *Mission Marvel*, page 14.

Revise/Practise/Apply   Word alert: whole   who

- Read each word in turn by saying the sounds and then blending the sounds to read the word. Check that children can recall the focus GPC.

What does it mean?
- Before we read today's story, we will work together to understand the meanings of some of the words we will read today.
- Read the words 'throttle' and 'jutting out' and their definitions with the children and check they understand what they mean.

Guided/group reading 16 mins

- Can you remember where Team X are and what they are doing there?
- Where in Macro Marvel's body do you think the BITE is hiding?
- Turn to page 15 and read the first chapter aloud as children follow silently in their books. Pause at the end of page 19.
- Look back at page 16. Did you notice the words 'dum-dum' were in italics? The author is telling us that these words represent the sound of the heart beating. How do you think we should say the words to sound like a heart beat? Let's try it together.
- From Chapter 2, page 20, ask children to continue reading the book quietly at their own pace. Listen in on each individual reader in turn.
- Expect children to decode successfully, without being prompted. They should recognise the GPC wh (/h/). As they read, use the Phonic record sheet to note any words that an individual misreads.
- If a child decodes a word incorrectly, encourage them to read it again, looking closely at the individual sounds. Then ask them to read the whole sentence again to check that it makes sense.

After reading 7 mins

- When each child has finished reading the story, ask them to turn to page 32. Explain that they need to find words and phrases that describe Hawkwing and the Virus-BITE's movements.
- What other words could you use to describe their movements? How would this affect the story?
- Share the examples children have found, e.g. Hawkwing: 'sped up' – page 20, 'jolted to a halt' – page 24, 'swerve' – page 25, 'dragged upwards' – page 27, 'soared' – page 28, 'hurtled' – page 31; Virus-BITE: 'swivelled' – page 20, 'darted' – page 22, 'crashed' – page 24.
- What did Macro Marvel do while Team X were inside his body? Put the labels into the correct order.
- Support children as they put the labels into the correct sequence by finding evidence in the story: snored – page 18, gave a huge jerk – page 25, coughed – page 28, swallowed – page 31.
- Now that Macro Marvel has swallowed Hawkwing, where do you think Team X will end up next?
- Encourage children to make predictions and think about what it will be like in Macro Marvel's stomach.

Takeaway: reading and writing 3 mins

- You are going to record your ideas about the book you have just finished on your reading log. There are some questions to get you thinking.
- Give each child PCM 101 and a copy of *Mission Marvel* to take away.

Race Against Time

Gold band
Marvel Towers zone
Book 52

Resources
- CODE tracker files
- Marvel Towers zone Book 52 *Race Against Time*
- Phonic record sheet – Gold band (page 29)
- PCM 102 Spelling challenge

Focus GPCs
(w)ar as in warm, (w)a as in water, a(lt) as in alternating, (w)a as in was

Team X word
Mini

Exploring vocabulary (What does it mean?)
stirred

The EYE of CODE

Introduction 3 mins
- Look at children's completed reading logs on PCM 101. (Takeaway from previous session.) Ask them if they would rather be with Mini or the others?

Word workout and Before reading 6 mins
💬 *Before we find out more about Mini and Macro Marvel, we will do a Word workout to get our reading and writing brains working.*

(See pages 47–49 for details and an explanation of the additional Word workout activities. If any children still need to practise oral blending, select 2–3 words from a previous book.)

- Turn to *Race Against Time*, page 4.

Revise/Practise/Apply	**Word alert:** warm water alternating was warned want swallowed

💬 *The most common way to spell /or/ is 'or'. In some words, where the /or/ sound comes after the letter 'w', we use the letters 'ar' as in 'warm' or 'a' as in 'water'.*

💬 *You already know the most common way to spell the short /o/ sound using the letter 'o'. In some words, where the /o/ sound comes after the letter 'w', we use the letter 'a' as in 'was'.*

- Look at the words 'warned', 'want' and 'swallowed'. Ask children to take turns to choose a word, say the sounds and then blend the sounds to read the word. Check that they remember the focus GPCs.

What does it mean?
💬 *Before we read today's story, we will work together to understand the meaning of one of the words we will read today.*

- Read the word 'stirred' and its definition with the children and check they understand what it means in the context of the story.

Reading the story 12 mins
💬 *How did Mini and Rex escape from the MITEs?* (Rex melted the chain that was holding him to a chair, then melted the lock of the door that was holding Mini captive and kept the MITEs back by breathing fire at them.)

💬 *What will make Macro Marvel better?* (Stopping the Virus-BITE.)

- Turn to page 5 and ask children to take turns reading a page each.
- Expect children to decode successfully, without being prompted. They should recognise the GPCs (w)ar (/or/), (w)a (/or/), a(lt) (/o/) and (w)a (/o/). As they read, use the Phonic record sheet to note any words that an individual misreads.
- Check that, after they decode and if the need arises, children reread a sentence to check that it makes sense, self-correcting if necessary.

After reading 6 mins
- Turn to page 13.

💬 *Is this statement true or false? 'CODE knows everything that goes on in Micro World.' Find some evidence for this in the story.*

- If children don't suggest it themselves, draw attention to page 8, where neither Marvel nor CODE know where Team X are.

💬 *There are three characters in this story who each speak in a different way. What do you think Mini, Marvel and CODE would sound like? Let's read part of the story again and try out different voices.*

- Reread pages 6–10, with three children taking the parts of Mini, Marvel and CODE while you narrate. Encourage them to use expression appropriate for that character.

💬 *What do you think will happen to Team X when Marvel swallows the water?* (Hawkwing will end up in his stomach.)

Takeaway: spelling 3 mins
- Explain that today's Takeaway is a spelling activity. Give each child PCM 102. They will need to identify the tricky parts in the words (from *Mission Marvel* and *Race Against Time*) and learn to spell them using Look, Cover, Remember, Write, Check.

Race Against Time

Gold band
Marvel Towers zone
Book 52

Resources
- CODE tracker files
- Marvel Towers zone Book 52 *Race Against Time*
- Phonic record sheet – Gold band (page 29)
- PCM 103 Reading log: Race Against Time
- PCM 104 Marvel Towers CODE words
- Marvel Towers zone Books 49–51

Focus GPCs
(w)ar as in warm, (w)a as in water, a(lt) as in alternating, (w)a as in was

Team X word
Mini

Exploring vocabulary (What does it mean?)
stomach acid

Additional, not yet decodable words
engine/s, coughed, moving, moved, great

Hold on Tight

Introduction and Before reading 4 mins

- Look at children's completed spelling challenges on PCM 102. (Takeaway from previous session.) Talk about the tricky parts in words and children's strategies for remembering them.
- *Team X still need to stop the Virus-BITE. Before we find out what happens next, we will do some activities to get us ready to read.*
- Turn to *Race Against Time*, page 14.

Revise/Practise/Apply	**Word alert:** towards water watch alter

- Read each word in turn by saying the sounds and then blending the sounds to read the word. Check that children can recall the focus GPCs.

What does it mean?
- *Before we read today's story, we will work together to understand the meaning of one of the phrases we will read today.*
- Read the phrase 'stomach acid' and its definition with children and check they understand what it means.

Guided/group reading 16 mins

- *How did Mini try to contact Team X? (She whispered in Marvel's ear.) Do you think they'll hear her?*
- *Can you remember which part of Macro Marvel Team X are heading for? (His stomach.)*
- Turn to page 15 and read the first chapter aloud as children follow silently in their books.
- *Did you notice that this chapter has the same events as the last story we read, but this time it's told from the point of view of Team X? We can see the effect of Marvel's actions. (E.g. he swallows water and Hawkwing gets washed away (page 16); Mini talks and Team X hear her (page 18).)*
- From Chapter 2, page 19, ask children to continue reading the book quietly at their own pace. Listen in on each individual reader in turn.
- Expect children to decode successfully, without being prompted. They should recognise the GPCs (w)ar (/or/), (w)a (/or/), a(lt) (/o/) and (w)a (/o/). As they read, use the Phonic record sheet to note any words that an individual misreads.
- If a child decodes a word incorrectly, encourage them to read it again, looking closely at the individual sounds. Then ask them to read the whole sentence again to check that it makes sense.

After reading 7 mins

- When children finish reading the story, ask them to turn to page 32. Give each child PCM 103 and ask them to work in pairs to discuss which Marvel Towers book they liked best. They can make notes on their reading logs.
- While all the children are doing this, work with each child individually as they read the list of invented CODE words (pseudo words) on page 32 of *Race Against Time*. Check that they can recall the GPCs and blend them to read words. Keep a record using PCM 104.
- *Team X have managed to save Macro Marvel by stopping the Virus-BITE, but their mission isn't finished yet. They've still got to stop CODE from shrinking the world.*

Takeaway: reading and writing 3 mins

- Look together at the remaining questions on PCM 103 and check that children understand what to do.
- Children can complete their reading logs at school or at home. They can also take their favourite Marvel Towers book away to share with someone.

97 Cards and labels

Challenge cards

Talk about Micro World.

Work with a partner and answer the questions.

1. Which zone did you like the most? Why?
2. Which ride would you like to go on? Why?
3. Which BITE was the most frightening? Why?

Talk about Micro World.

Work with a partner and answer the questions.

1. Which zone did you like the most? Why?
2. Which ride would you like to go on? Why?
3. Which BITE was the most frightening? Why?

'Ask me about' labels

Ask me about the human body.

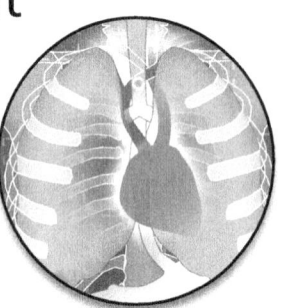

Ask me about the human body.

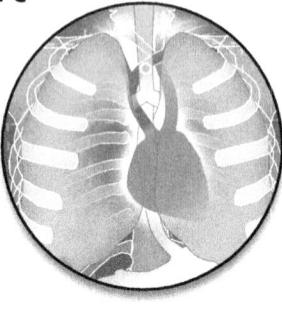

Ask me about the human body.

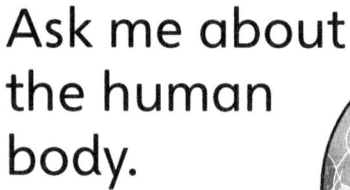

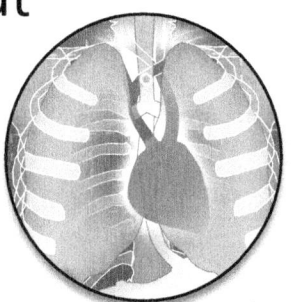

Ask me about the human body.

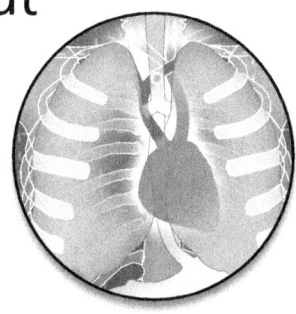

Gold band • Marvel Towers zone • **Cards and labels**

Children follow instructions on the cards to complete the activity.

Name _____ Date _____

Reading log: A Shock for Mini

Read the questions and write your ideas about the story.

1. What do you think was the most important event?
   _____
   _____

2. Write a question to ask one of the characters.
   _____
   _____

3. How will Team X get inside Macro Marvel's body?
   _____
   _____
   _____

4. Did anything puzzle you? Write down any questions you have about this book. _____
   _____
   _____
   _____

Spelling challenge

Follow the steps to spell the words.

1. Look at the word. Find the tricky part.
2. Cover the word. Say each sound. Write the word.
3. Check it is correct. ✓ or ✗
4. Write the word again.

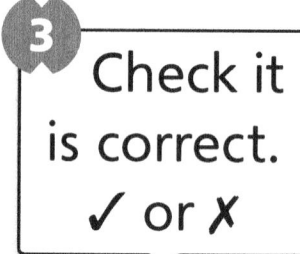

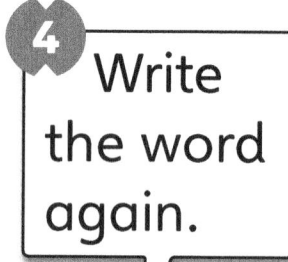

Look	Write	Check	Write
could			
would			
should			
couldn't			
wouldn't			
wrist			
wriggled			
wrinkling			
rhubarb			
rhythm			

Name _____ Date _____

Reading log: A BITE Inside

Read the questions and write your ideas about the story.

1. Where did the story take place? Describe it.

_____

_____

_____

2. If you were Mini, what message would you send to Team X? _____

_____

_____

_____

3. Did anything puzzle you? Write down any questions you have about this book. _____

_____

_____

_____

Gold band ● Marvel Towers zone ● **Reading log**

Children read the questions and write answers to them.

Reading log: Mission Marvel

Read the questions and write your ideas about the story.

1. Did you enjoy this book? Why? _____

2. Would you rather be with Mini, inside the Control Room, or with the others, chasing the BITE? Why?

3. Did anything puzzle you? Write down any questions you have about this book. _____

Name _____ Date _____

Spelling challenge

Follow the steps to spell the words.

1 Look at the word. Find the tricky part.

2 Cover the word. Say each sound. Write the word.

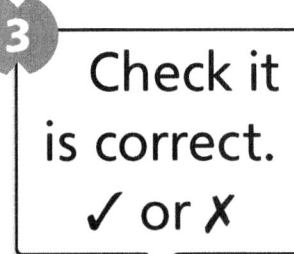

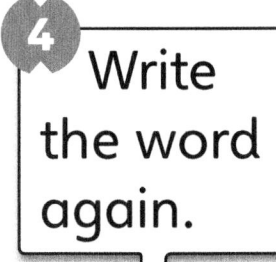

3 Check it is correct. ✓ or ✗

4 Write the word again.

Look	Write	Check	Write
whole			
who			
hands			
hidden			
warm			
warned			
water			
alternating			
want			
was			

Reading log: Race Against Time

Read the questions and write your ideas about the story.

1. Which Marvel Towers book did you like best? Why?

_____

_____

_____

2. Look back at the questions you wrote in your reading logs. Write down any answers you have now.

_____

_____

_____

3. Team X and Mini have still got to stop CODE. What do you think will happen next? _____

_____

_____

_____

Marvel Towers CODE words

These words are a code. Can you help us read them?

kive ☐	pife ☐	whosk ☐
treelt ☐	koopie ☐	praff ☐
fiep ☐	laves ☐	rhem ☐

CODE's Countdown

Gold band
CODE Control zone
Book 53

Resources
- Zone map
- CODE Control zone Book 53 *CODE's Countdown*
- Flashcards: s, ie
- Phonic record sheet – Gold band (page 29)
- Card 1 from **PCM 105 Challenge cards** for each child

Practice GPCs
s /s/ as in parts, s /z/ as in watches, ie /ee/ as in babies

Focus suffixes
-s, -es, -ies

Team X word
Mini

Exploring vocabulary (What does it mean?)
lurking, sneered

Secret in the Shadows

Introduction 3 mins
- If a child is new to CODE, give them their CODE tracker file. Explain that it's a special file to track Team X and Mini's progress through the Micro World zones. Ask them to complete PCM 3 (from *Teaching and Assessment Handbook 1*) as a cover sheet for their file.
- Look at the zone map (on page 4 of *CODE's Countdown*) and use it to recap the story. Explain that Team X and Mini are at the centre of Micro World.
- Ask children to recall what happened in the last story.

Word workout and Before reading 5 mins
- *Before we start reading, we will have a short Word workout to get our reading and writing brains working.*
  (See pages 47–49 for details and an explanation of the flashcard activity and other Word workout activities. If any children still need to practise oral blending, select 2–3 words from a previous book.)

  Revise/Practise Flashcards: s (/s/ and /z/), ie (/ee/)

- *You already know that 's' can be pronounced /s/ as in 'parts' or /z/ as in 'watches', and 'ie' can be pronounced /ee/ as in 'babies'. We are going to read words with these sounds at the end.*
- Turn to *CODE's Countdown*, page 5.

  Apply Word alert: BITEs heroes enemies

- *The letters -s, -es and -ies are suffixes – something added to a word to change how it works. Look out for more of these as you are reading.*
- *In this case, the suffixes have been added to show these words are plurals (more than one of something).*

  What does it mean?
- *Before we read today's story, we will work together to understand the meaning of some of the words we will read today.*
- Read the words 'lurking' and 'sneered' and their definitions with the children and check they understand what they mean.

Reading the story 12 mins
- *Can you remember what CODE's goal is?* (To shrink the world.)
- *This story is called 'Secret in the Shadows'. What do you think the secret might be?*
- Ask children to take turns reading a page aloud.
- Expect children to decode successfully, without being prompted. As they read, use the Phonic record sheet to note words that an individual misreads and to check they can correctly read words with the focus suffixes.
- Check that, after they decode and if the need arises, children reread a sentence to check that it makes sense, self-correcting if necessary.

After reading 7 mins
- Turn to page 13.
- *Look back at the story to find clues about CODE's character. For example, on page 6, it says 'CODE's red eye flashed angrily' so we know that, unlike a normal computer, CODE has feelings and can show its anger.*
- *Are these sentences true or false? Use evidence from the story to explain why.*
- Read the sentences on page 13. If necessary, draw attention to page 6: CODE is angry with Team X; CODE is not talking to itself; CODE's shrinking rays are almost fully charged.
- *What do you think CODE's secret weapon is?*
- Encourage children to contribute their ideas, particularly drawing on their knowledge of ways CODE has attacked Team X and Mini so far.

Takeaway: talking 3 mins
- Give each child Card 1 from PCM 105.
- *What do you think CODE's voice sounds like? Work in pairs to read pages 6–9, taking it in turns so that one person is CODE and the other is the narrator. Record your reading, check you are happy with it, then perform it to someone.*

CODE's Countdown

Gold band
CODE Control zone
Book 53

Resources
- CODE Control zone Book 53 *CODE's Countdown*
- Phonic record sheet – Gold band (page 29)
- CODE tracker files with PCM 106 Reading log: *CODE's Countdown*

Practice GPCs
s /s/ as in parts, s /z/ as in watches, ie /ee/ as in babies

Focus suffixes
-s, -es, -ies

Team X word
Mini

Exploring vocabulary (What does it mean?)
air vent, desperation

Additional, not yet decodable words
sure, surely, enormous, two, shone, move, millions

The Secret Revealed

Introduction and Before reading 4 mins
- Listen to one pair of children reading pages 6–9 of *CODE's Countdown*, using the voice they practised for CODE. (Takeaway from previous session.)
- Ask the other children if that's how they imagined CODE's voice would sound.
- 💬 *Before we read, we will do some activities to get us ready for the next story.*
- Turn to *CODE's Countdown*, page 14.

Revise/Practise/Apply — **Word alert:** parts   watches   bodies

💬 *The letters -s, -es and -ies are suffixes – something added to a word to change how it works. The suffixes show that there is more than one of something (plural). Look out for these when you are reading the story.*

What does it mean?
💬 *Before we read today's story, we will work together to understand the meaning of some of the words we will read today.*
- Read the words 'air vent' and 'desperation' and their definitions with the children and check they understand what they mean.

Guided/group reading 16 mins
- 💬 *What do you think Team X will do next?*
- 💬 *They are very close to CODE now. Do you think Macro Marvel will be able to tell Team X how to defeat CODE?*
- Turn to page 15 and read the first chapter aloud as children follow silently in their books. Demonstrate how to use appropriate expression for different characters.
- From Chapter 2, page 19, ask each child to continue reading the book quietly at their own pace. Listen in on each individual in turn.
- Expect children to decode successfully, without being prompted. As they read, use the Phonic record sheet to note words that an individual misreads and to check they can correctly read words with the focus suffixes.
- If a child decodes incorrectly or is puzzled by a word, encourage them to read the whole word again, looking closely at the sounds in the word. They should then read the whole sentence again to check it makes sense.

After reading 7 mins
- When each child has finished reading the story, ask them to turn to page 32. Explain that they need to look closely at the picture of the BITE on page 24 and spot all the different BITEs that have been used to make it.
- When all children have finished reading, talk about the different methods of attack that the BITE can use against Team X.
- 💬 *Look at the four pictures and use them to help you remember what happened and tell the story from Tiger's point of view, e.g. "I was so excited about sliding down the air vent, but then …".*
- 💬 *At the end of the story, Max asked Mini and her dad for help to defeat the BITE. What advice do you think they will give?*

Takeaway: reading and writing 3 mins
- 💬 *You are going to start a reading log about the CODE Control books. There are some questions to get you thinking and you can write your own ideas about the story.*
- Give each child PCM 106 and a copy of *CODE's Countdown* to take away.

The Last BITE
Gold band
CODE Control zone
Book 54

The Mega-BITE

Introduction 3 mins
- Ask one or two children to choose a character and explain what they did in the last book. (Takeaway from previous session.)

Word workout and Before reading 5 mins
💬 *Before we start reading, we are going to have a short Word workout to get our reading and writing brains working.*

(See pages 47–49 for details and an explanation of the flashcard activity and other Word workout activities. If any children still need to practise oral blending, select 2–3 words from a previous book.)

Revise/Practise Flashcard: ed (/d/ and /t/)

💬 *You already know that 'ed' can be pronounced /d/ as in 'pulled'. In some words it is pronounced /t/ as in 'jumped'. We are going to read some words with 'ed' at the end.*

- Turn to *The Last BITE*, page 4.

Apply Word alert: needed   looked   opened

💬 *The letters -ed are called a suffix – something added to a word to change how it works. This time the suffix -ed changes action words (verbs) to show that the action has already happened (past tense). Look out for words with this suffix when you are reading.*

What does it mean?
💬 *Before we read today's story, we will work together to understand the meaning of some of the words we will read today.*
- Read the word 'password' and its definition with the children and check they understand what it means.

Reading the story 12 mins
💬 *Can you remember why Mini and Marvel can't access information on the computer?* (Because they need to crack the code first.)
💬 *Why does CODE want to shrink everyone?* (To keep people safe. CODE believes that by making people small they won't need so much food or make so much pollution.)
- Turn to page 5 and ask children to take turns reading a page aloud.
- Expect children to decode successfully, without being prompted. As they read, use the Phonic record sheet to note words that an individual misreads and to check they can correctly read words with the focus suffix.
- Check that, after they decode and if the need arises, children reread a sentence to check that it makes sense, self-correcting if necessary.

After reading 7 mins
- Turn to page 13.
💬 *Can you explain what happened when Mini was trying to crack the code words? Look at page 6 to help you fill in the gaps in the sentence: '**First** a MITE tapped the control panel **and then** [some letters turned red] **so that** Mini [could work out the password]'.*
💬 *Find three things that make the Mega-BITE so dangerous. Which do you think is the most important? Complete this sentence: 'The Mega-BITE is the most dangerous BITE of all because …'*
💬 *How do you think Team X and Mini will stop the Mega-BITE? What have they done with all the other BITEs? Will they be able to do the same this time?*
- Draw out the idea that Team X and Mini won't be able to just pull the CODE key out as usual because it's buried inside the Mega-BITE's body.

Takeaway: spelling 3 mins
- Explain that today's Takeaway is a spelling challenge. Give each child PCM 107. They will need to identify the spelling patterns of the suffixes they have been looking at and learn to spell the words using Look, Cover, Remember, Write, Check.

Resources
- CODE tracker files
- Flashcard: ed
- CODE Control zone Book 54 *The Last BITE*
- Phonic record sheet – Gold band (page 29)
- PCM 107 Spelling challenge

Practice GPCs
ed /d/ as in pulled, ed /t/ as in jumped

Focus suffix
-ed

Team X word
Mini

Exploring vocabulary (What does it mean?)
password

The Last BITE
Gold band
CODE Control zone
Book 54

Resources
- CODE tracker files
- CODE Control zone Book 54 *The Last BITE*
- Phonic record sheet – Gold band (page 29)
- PCM 108 Reading log: The Last BITE

Practice GPCs
ed /d/ as in pulled, ed /t/ as in jumped

Focus suffix
-ed

Team X word
Mini

Exploring vocabulary (What does it mean?)
ear-splitting, hoisted

Additional, not yet decodable words
proving, break, tremendous, done, moved, hey, moving

Crack the BITE

Introduction and Before reading 4 mins

- Look at children's completed spelling challenges on PCM 107. (Takeaway from previous session.) Talk about the tricky parts in words and children's strategies for remembering them.
- 💬 *Before we find out what happens next to Team X and Mini, we will do some activities to get us ready to read.*
- Turn to *The Last BITE*, page 14.

Revise/Practise/Apply	**Word alert:** gasped trapped cried

- 💬 *Do you remember the suffix -ed that we can add to an action word (verb) to show that the action has already happened (past tense)?*
- 💬 *When the base word ends in 'y', the 'y' changes to 'i' before the -ed is added – so words that end in 'ied' also show that the action has already happened. Look out for these when you are reading.*

What does it mean?
- 💬 *Before we read today's story, we will work together to understand the meaning of some of the words we will read today.*
- Read the words 'ear-splitting' and 'hoisted' and their definitions with the children and check they understand what they mean.

Guided/group reading 16 mins

- 💬 *Team X are trapped. Can you remember where they are?* (In the Central Chamber with the Mega-BITE.)
- 💬 *What do you think Mini's idea might be for defeating the Mega-BITE?*
- Turn to page 15 and read the first chapter aloud as children follow silently in their books.
- From Chapter 2, page 19, ask each child to continue reading the book quietly at their own pace. Listen in on each individual in turn.
- Expect children to decode successfully, without being prompted. As they read, use the Phonic record sheet to note words that an individual misreads and to check they can correctly read words with the focus suffix.
- If a child decodes incorrectly or is puzzled by a word, encourage them to read the whole word again, looking closely at the sounds in the word. They should then read the whole sentence again to check it makes sense.

After reading 7 mins

- When each child has finished reading, ask them to turn to page 32. Explain that they need to find different words on pages 20–22 that describe how the Mega-BITE moved when it was trying to reach the CODE keys.
- When all children have finished reading, share the examples they have found: 'shuddered', 'trembling', 'twist and turn', 'straining', 'reached', 'pulled', 'tugging', 'rocked back and forth', 'broke off', 'split', 'clattered'.
- 💬 *Imagine you are Max, removing the CODE key from the Mega-BITE. What would you say? What are you thinking? How are you feeling?*
- Explain that, in order to answer the questions, children need to think about Max's character. (He is the team leader, is brave and always encourages the others.)
- 💬 *Can you shrink the story down to just four sentences? Think about the most important event in each chapter.*
- Support children as they identify key events and compose their sentences.

Takeaway: reading and writing 3 mins

- 💬 *You are going to record your ideas about the book you have just finished on a reading log.*
- Give each child PCM 108 and a copy of *The Last BITE*.

Eye to Eye
Gold band
CODE Control zone
Book 55

Resources
- CODE tracker files
- Flashcard: ng
- CODE Control zone Book 55 *Eye to Eye*
- Phonic record sheet – Gold band (page 29)
- Card 2 from **PCM 105 Challenge cards** for each child

Practice GPC
ng as in rang

Focus suffix
-ing

Team X word
Mini

Exploring vocabulary (What does it mean?)
paced

The Master Key

Introduction 3 mins
- Look at children's completed reading logs on PCM 108 (Takeaway from previous session) and ask them to share their ideas about Mini and Marvel's next set of instructions for Team X.
- Briefly discuss how, at the end of the last story, Ant talked about Team X having to face CODE.
- *How do you think Team X must be feeling now?*

Word workout and Before reading 5 mins
- *Let's do a short Word workout to get our reading and writing brains working.* (See pages 47–49 for details and an explanation of the flashcard activity and other Word workout activities. If any children still need to practise oral blending, select 2–3 words from a previous book.)

Revise/Practise Flashcard: ng

- *We're going to read some words that end with the /ng/ sound.*
- Turn to *Eye to Eye*, page 4.

Apply Word alert: knowing dazzling going

- *The letters -ing are another suffix – something added to a word to change how it works. This suffix changes action words (verbs) to show that the action is happening now (present tense). Look out for words with this suffix when you are reading the story.*

What does it mean?
- *Before we read today's story, we will work together to understand the meaning of one of the words we will read today.*
- Read the word 'paced' and its definition with the children and check they understand what it means.

Reading the story 12 mins
- *What do Team X and Mini still have to do?* (Stop CODE.)
- *How many CODE keys have they collected?* (14 – one from each zone and two extras from the Virus-BITE and the Mega-BITE.)
- Turn to page 5 and ask children to take turns reading a page aloud.
- Expect children to decode successfully, without being prompted. As they read, use the Phonic record sheet to note words that an individual misreads and to check they can correctly read words with the focus suffix.
- Check that, after they decode and if the need arises, children reread a sentence to check that it makes sense, self-correcting if necessary.

After reading 7 mins
- Turn to page 13.
- *How do you make and use the Master key? Use information from the story to complete a set of instructions.*
- Support children as they use the words to complete the instructions, e.g. '**First** [collect all the CODE keys]. **Next** [slot them together to make the Master key]. **Finally** [insert the Master key in the top of CODE].'
- Look at the picture of Tiger holding two CODE keys.
- *Choose a word to describe the CODE keys that Tiger is holding. Can you think of any other describing words (adjectives) you could use?*
- Encourage children to experiment, deciding which adjectives make sense, which are funny, and so on.
- *At the end of the story, Team X were trapped in CODE Control. Imagine what they could hear and see. How did they feel?*
- Ask children to reread page 12 and look for information about what Team X could hear and see, then make inferences about how they were feeling.

Takeaway: talking 3 mins
- Give each child Card 2 from PCM 105 to take away. Challenge them to choose their favourite character and think about all the adventures they've had in Micro World, using the books to help them. They can then tell someone at home or at school about that character.

Eye to Eye
Gold band
CODE Control zone
Book 55

Resources
- CODE Control zone Book 55 *Eye to Eye*
- Phonic record sheet – Gold band (page 29)
- CODE tracker files with PCM 109 Reading log: *Eye to Eye*

Practice GPC
ng as in rang

Focus suffix
-ing

Team X word
Mini

Exploring vocabulary (What does it mean?)
dazzled

Additional, not yet decodable words
minutes, moving, deliberately, removed, built, move, shone, great, serious

Steps of Terror

Introduction and Before reading 4 mins
- Ask children which character they talked about in the Takeaway from the previous session. Can they use one adjective to describe them?
- *Before we find out how Team X will face CODE, we will do some activities to get us ready to read.*
- Turn to *Eye to Eye*, page 14.

Revise/Practise/Apply	Word alert: keeping whirring talking

- *Remember the suffix -ing. This is what we add to an action word (verb) to show that the action is happening now (present tense).*
- *In words that end in 'e', we need to take off the 'e' before adding -ing, for example make/making.*

What does it mean?
- *Before we read today's story, we will work together to understand the meaning of one of the words we will read today.*
- Read the word 'dazzled' and its definition with the children and check they understand what it means.

Guided/group reading 16 mins
- *What did Team X make in the last story?* (The Master key.)
- *How do you think they will escape from CODE?*
- Turn to page 15 and read the first chapter aloud as children follow silently in their books.
- From Chapter 2, page 20, ask each child to continue reading the book quietly at their own pace. Listen in on each individual in turn.
- Expect children to decode successfully, without being prompted. As they read, use the Phonic record sheet to note words that an individual misreads and to check they can correctly read words with the focus suffix.
- If a child decodes incorrectly or is puzzled by a word, encourage them to read the whole word again, looking closely at the sounds in the word. They should then read the whole sentence again to check it makes sense.

After reading 7 mins
- When each child finishes reading, ask them to turn to page 32 and use the pictures to remind them what happened so they can summarise and retell the story from Cat's point of view.
- When all children have finished reading, ask a child who finished earlier to retell Cat's story.
- *How would you describe CODE? Read the list of describing words (adjectives) and decide which ones are best. Can you find evidence in the story to back up your choices?*
- Demonstrate this, for example:
- *CODE is dreadful because it fills people with dread, like Cat who trembled when she heard CODE speak (page 16) and felt a 'sickening sense of dread' (page 30) because they hadn't stopped CODE.*
- *Everything seems hopeless at the end of this story. Team X tried their best, but they haven't managed to stop CODE. What do you think will happen next?*
- Encourage children to suggest their own ideas based on what they have read so far.

Takeaway: reading and writing 3 mins
- *You are going to complete a reading log to record your ideas about the book you have just finished reading.*
- Give each child PCM 109 and a copy of *Eye to Eye*.

Stop CODE!
Gold band
CODE Control zone
Book 56

Resources
- CODE tracker files
- Flashcard: y
- CODE Control zone Book 56 *Stop CODE!*
- Phonic record sheet – Gold band (page 29)
- PCM 110 Spelling challenge

Practice GPC
y (at the end of a word): /ee/ as in shiny

Focus suffixes
-y, -ly

Exploring vocabulary (What does it mean?)
hastily

The Transporter

Introduction 3 mins
- Look at children's completed reading logs on PCM 109 (Takeaway from previous session) and share their plans for stopping CODE. Encourage them to ask each other questions about their ideas.

Word workout and Before reading 5 mins
- *Before we find out what happens next, we are going to have a short Word workout to get our reading and writing brains working.*
  (See pages 47–49 for details and an explanation of the flashcard activity and other Word workout activities. If any children still need to practise oral blending, select 2–3 words from a previous book.)

  Revise/Practise **Flashcard:** y (/ee/)

- *You already know that 'y' can be pronounced /ee/ as in 'shiny'. We are going to read words with this sound at the end of them.*
- Turn to *Stop CODE!*, page 4.

  Apply **Word alert:** uneasy shiny desperately bravely

- *The letter -y is another suffix. It changes words to describing words (adjectives).*
- *The letters -ly are a suffix, too. They change describing words (adjectives) into new words to describe how something took place (adverbs).*
- *Look out for these suffixes when you are reading the story.*

  What does it mean?
- *Before we read today's story, we will work together to understand the meaning of one of the words we will read today.*
- Read the word 'hastily' and its definition with the children and check they understand what it means.

Reading the story 12 mins
- *Things were looking bad for Team X at the end of the last story. Can you remember how long it will be before CODE shrinks the world? (10 minutes.)*
- *Would any of the plans you made for stopping CODE work in just 10 minutes? How might Team X stop CODE?*
- Turn to page 5 and ask children to take turns reading a page aloud.
- Expect children to decode successfully, without being prompted. As they read, use the Phonic record sheet to note words that an individual misreads and to check they can correctly read words with the focus suffixes.
- Check that, after they decode and if the need arises, children reread a sentence to check that it makes sense, self-correcting if necessary.

After reading 7 mins
- Turn to page 13.
- *Read the sentences about Mini and decide which are true and which are false.*
- Help children find evidence for each answer, e.g. Mini thinks quickly because she came up with a new plan (page 6); she is brave because she volunteered to use an untested Transporter (page 12); she doesn't let her dad do all the work because she offered to be transported instead of him (page 12).
- *Do you think Mini has changed since she met Team X? She has always been determined to rescue her dad, but do you think she has become braver?*
- Encourage children to reflect on Mini's role and the things she has done since reaching Marvel Towers, e.g. being the first to find Marvel; never giving up.
- *Look back at page 12. What did Marvel say about letting Mini use the Transporter? Imagine that you are him. What did he think? How did he feel?*
- *For example, it says that Marvel felt uneasy, which shows how worried he was. He might have thought Mini would disappear.*

Takeaway: spelling 3 mins
- Explain that today's Takeaway is a spelling challenge. Give each child PCM 110. They will need to identify the spelling patterns of the suffixes they have been looking at and learn to spell the words using Look, Cover, Remember, Write, Check.

Stop CODE!
Gold band
CODE Control zone
Book 56

Resources
- CODE tracker files
- CODE Control zone Book 56 Stop CODE!
- Phonic record sheet – Gold band (page 29)
- Any available Project X CODE books
- PCM 111 A Micro World Adventure
- PCM 112 Reading log: Stop CODE!

Practice GPC
y (at the end of a word): /ee/ as in shiny

Focus suffixes
-y, -ly

Exploring vocabulary (What does it mean?)
recognisable

Additional, not yet decodable words
minutes, furiously, we're, done, anxious, none, gone, goodbye, sure

Stop CODE!

Introduction and Before reading 4 mins
- Look at children's completed spelling challenges on PCM 110. (Takeaway from previous session.) Talk about the tricky parts in words and children's strategies for remembering them.
- *Before we find out whether Team X and Mini can defeat CODE, we will do a short Word workout to get our reading and writing brains working.*
- Turn to *Stop CODE!*, page 14.

Revise/Practise/Apply	Word alert: scary joyfully proudly

- *Do you remember the suffix -y? This is what we add to a word to change it to a describing word (adjective).*
- *The -ly suffix is added to a describing word (adjective) to show how something took place (adverb). Look out for more words with these suffixes when you are reading.*

What does it mean?
- *Before we read today's story, we will work together to understand the meaning of one of the words we will read today.*
- Read the word 'recognisable' and its definition with the children and check they understand what it means.

Guided/group reading 16 mins
- *What sort of danger is Team X in?* (They are trapped in CODE Control with CODE.)
- *What are Mini and Rex taking to Team X?* (The two extra CODE keys.) *Do you think Mini's plan will work?*
- Turn to page 15 and read the first chapter aloud as children follow silently in their books.
- From Chapter 2, page 19, ask each child to continue reading the book quietly at their own pace. Listen in on each individual in turn.
- Expect children to decode successfully, without being prompted. As they read, use the Phonic record sheet to note words that an individual misreads and to check they can correctly read words with the focus suffixes.
- If a child decodes incorrectly or is puzzled by a word, encourage them to read the whole word again, looking closely at the sounds in the word. They should then read the whole sentence again to check it makes sense.

After reading 7 mins
- When each child finishes reading, ask them to turn to page 32 and think about how Tiger felt about leaving Micro World, and which rides they would try if they went to Micro World.
- When all the children have finished reading, listen to their suggestions.
- *That was an exciting end to Team X's mission! Can you shrink the story down to four sentences? Think about the most important event in each chapter.*
- *Team X and Mini have finally stopped CODE, but is it really all over? Did you spot any clues in the story that suggest CODE might not be defeated?*
- Help children identify clues, e.g. Team X are uncertain when Marvel says that CODE will never go wrong again (page 28); Max is uneasy when he sees CODE's red eye glinting horribly inside the Master key (pages 24 and 31).
- Finish this final session with a celebration. Look together at all the books children have read and talk about their favourites. Help children reflect on their achievements and think about their next targets. Children can use PCM 111 to keep a record.

Takeaway: reading and writing 3 mins
- *There is one more reading log to help you think back over all the Project X CODE stories and make up a new adventure for Team X.*
- Give each child PCM 112 to take away.

Challenge cards

Card 1

Read in CODE's voice.

1. Work with a partner.
2. Practise reading pages 6–9 of *CODE's Countdown*. One person is CODE and the other is the narrator.
3. When you are ready, perform your reading to someone else.

Read in CODE's voice.

1. Work with a partner.
2. Practise reading pages 6–9 of *CODE's Countdown*. One person is CODE and the other is the narrator.
3. When you are ready, perform your reading to someone else.

Card 2

Talk about your favourite character.

1. Choose your favourite character and think about the different things they have done in Micro World. Use the books to help you.
2. Tell someone about the character you chose.

Talk about your favourite character.

1. Choose your favourite character and think about the different things they have done in Micro World. Use the books to help you.
2. Tell someone about the character you chose.

Reading log: CODE's Countdown

Read the questions and write your ideas about the story.

1. What do you think of CODE's secret weapon?

_____

_____

_____

2. Choose one character. Explain what they did in this book. _____

_____

_____

_____

3. Did anything puzzle you? Write down any questions you have about this book. _____

_____

_____

_____

Spelling challenge

Follow the steps to spell the words.

1. Look at the word. Find the tricky part.
2. Cover the word. Say each sound. Write the word.
3. Check it is correct. ✓ or ✗
4. Write the word again.

Look	Write	Check	Write
heads			
keys			
watches			
enemies			
bodies			
needed			
sighed			
pulled			
turned			
opened			

Reading log: The Last BITE

Read the questions and write your ideas about the story.

1. Which character would you like to be? Why?

2. What do you think Mini and Marvel will tell Team X to do next?

3. Did anything puzzle you? Write down any questions you have about this book.

Name _____ Date _____

Reading log: Eye to Eye

Read the questions and write your ideas about the story.

1. What were the key events in this book? _____
   _____
   _____
   _____
   _____

2. Make up your own plan for stopping CODE. _____
   _____
   _____
   _____
   _____

3. Did anything puzzle you? Write down any questions you have about this book. _____
   _____
   _____
   _____

Gold band • CODE Control zone • **Reading log**

Children read the questions and write answers to them.

Spelling challenge

Follow the steps to spell the words.

1. Look at the word. Find the tricky part.
2. Cover the word. Say each sound. Write the word.
3. Check it is correct. ✓ or ✗
4. Write the word again.

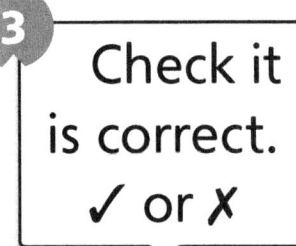

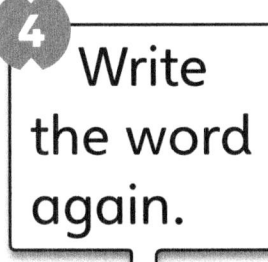

Look	Write	Check	Write
lifting			
going			
making			
blinding			
talking			
shiny			
uneasy			
desperately			
hastily			
bravely			

Children spell words with suffixes from *Eye to Eye* and *Stop CODE!*

A Micro World Adventure

> Well done! You have completed your Micro World mission!

I have read _____ books.

I feel proud I can _____

_____

The best zone was _____

My favourite character was:

☐ ☐ ☐ ☐ ☐ ☐

The scariest BITE was _____

because _____

The ride I would like to go on is _____

The next book I will read is _____

_____

Reading log: Stop CODE!

Read the questions and write your ideas about the story.

1. What was worrying Max at the end of this book?

2. Which CODE Control book did you like best? Why?

3. CODE strikes again! Plan a new adventure for Team X.

OXFORD
UNIVERSITY PRESS

Great Clarendon Street, Oxford, OX2 6DP,
United Kingdom

Oxford University Press is a department of the University of Oxford.
It furthers the University's objective of excellence in research, scholarship,
and education by publishing worldwide. Oxford is a registered trade mark of
Oxford University Press in the UK and in certain other countries

© Oxford University Press 2012

The moral rights of the authors have been asserted.

First Edition published in 2012

All rights reserved. No part of this publication may be reproduced, stored in
a retrieval system, or transmitted, in any form or by any means, without the
prior permission in writing of Oxford University Press, or as expressly permitted
by law, by licence or under terms agreed with the appropriate reprographics
rights organization. Enquiries concerning reproduction outside the scope of the
above should be sent to the Rights Department, Oxford University Press, at the
address above.

You must not circulate this work in any other form
and you must impose this same condition on any acquirer

British Library Cataloguing in Publication Data
Data available

978-0-19-834069-0

5 7 9 10 8 6

Paper used in the production of this book is a natural, recyclable product
made from wood grown in sustainable forests. The manufacturing process conforms
to the environmental regulations of the country of origin.

Printed in Great Britain by Bell and Bain Ltd, Glasgow

CD-ROM: Manufactured in Great Britain by Mediaplant Ltd

Acknowledgements
p5 educationphotos.co.uk/walmsley
p13 [1] Relative Effectiveness of Reading Practice or Word-Level Instruction in
Supplemental Tutoring: How Text Matters, Patricia F. Vadasy, Elizabeth A. Sanders and Julia A. Peyton

Character illustrations by Jonatronix Ltd, Senior Art Director: Jon Stuart, 3D artist: Sean Frisby
Map illustration by Mads Berg
Series editors: Maureen Lewis, Di Hatchett
Phonics consultant: Marilyn Joyce
Teaching notes written by Rachael Sutherland
Project X concept by Rod Theodorou and Emma Lynch

**The publisher wishes to thank the following schools for their valuable
contribution to the trialling and development of Project X CODE:**

Old Know Junior School, Birmingham; Lacewood Primary School, Rotherham;
Thornhill Primary School, Southampton; Wilmington Primary School, Wilmington;
Hursthead Junior School, Cheadle; Burton Green Primary School, York

The publisher wishes to thank St Thomas of Canterbury Junior School, Brentwood
for taking part in the Professional Development films.